The Follies of
Globalisation Theory

The Follies of Globalisation Theory

Polemical Essays

———◆———

JUSTIN ROSENBERG

VERSO

London • New York

First published by Verso 2000
© Justin Rosenberg 2000
All rights reserved

The moral rights of the author have been asserted

Verso
UK: 6 Meard Street, London W1V 3HR
USA: 180 Varick Street, New York, NY 10014–4606

Verso is the imprint of New Left Books
www.versobooks.com

ISBN 1–85984–611–4

British Library Cataloguing in Publication Data
A catalogue record for this book is available from the British Library

Library of Congress Cataloging-in-Publication Data
A catalog record for this book is available from the Library of Congress

Typeset in New Baskerville by M Rules
Printed by Biddles Ltd, Guildford and King's Lynn

Für Beate

Johnson exclaimed (smiling,) 'Prosaical rogues! next time I write, I'll make both space and time pant.'

Boswell, *Life of Johnson*

Contents

Acknowledgements   xi

1   Introduction: The Problem of Globalisation Theory   1
     The General Problem   2
     'International Relations' and Globalisation Theory   9

2   Scholte's Folly   17
     Introduction   17
     A Definitional Achievement   21
     When Was the Westphalian System?   27

3   Rob Walker: Philosophical Backstop?   45
     Introduction   45
     Ontological Assumptions   50
     Space and Modernity   54
     Why Space?   61
     The Problematic of the International   65

**4   Giddens' *Consequences of Modernity*: Sociological
     Foundations?**   87
     Introduction   87
     Making the Break   91

Forward or Back?   100
Confusion in the Ranks   115
The Argument Regroups   125
Hide and Seek with Space and Time   132

5   **Conclusion: The Collapsing Temple of Globalisation
     Theory**   157

     Notes   167
     Bibliography   193
     Index   201

Acknowledgements

I owe a considerable debt to the many friends, colleagues and acquaintances who have helped me with encouragement, criticism and advice while I was writing this book. Julian Saurin inadvertently triggered the whole project by setting *The Consequences of Modernity* as a required reading for a research workshop at the University of Sussex. Parts of chapter 4 were presented as a paper at the International Studies Association Conference held in Los Angeles in March 2000. For helpful comments on that paper, I am grateful to Alex Colas, Stephen Howe, Branwen Gruffydd Jones, Mark Lacy, John MacLean, Martin Shaw, Georg Sørensen and Ted Tapper. Others who gave their advice and support include Gareth Dale, Tom Hickey, Nick Rennger and Neil Stammers. Meanwhile, Simon Bromley, Paul Cammack, Gregory Elliott and Fred Halliday all read a large part of the work at a late stage and helped to give it a greater clarity of focus. To all of these, my thanks. The first, last, largest and happiest debt of all is to my wife Beate. To her this book is dedicated, with love.

1

Introduction: The Problem of Globalisation Theory

'Globalisation', wrote Anthony Giddens in 1990, is 'a term which must have a key position in the lexicon of the social sciences.'[1] If so, then by the time he rose to deliver the first of his Reith Lectures on the subject in 1999 he would have had considerable grounds for satisfaction.[2] For the progress of that term in the intervening decade has been little short of spectacular. In academic writings and government policy statements, in the journalistic media and in popular consciousness, the claim that the world is becoming unified as never before seems to have established a powerful hold. Few expressions of this claim could compete with the *International Herald Tribune*, which startled its readers one October morning with the headline: 'Globalization Vaults into Reality'.[3] Yet in their own way the intellectual implications imputed to the idea in many academic writings have been no less dramatic. Globalisation is said to signal not only a truly basic social change – 'the supplanting of modernity with globality'[4] – but also, as a result of this change, the redundancy of some of the founding ideas of classical social theory, extending even to the very concept of 'society' itself. Even more dramatically, globalisation has necessitated a wholesale 'spatialization of social theory'[5] on the basis of a 'retrospective discovery'[6] of the centrality of speed of communication in the constitution of social orders:

> It suddenly seems clear that the divisions of the continents and of the globe as a whole were the function of distances made once imposingly real thanks to the primitiveness of transport and the hardships of travel. . . . 'distance' is a social product; its length varies depending on the speed with which it may be overcome. . . . All other socially produced factors of constitution, separation and the maintenance of collective identities – like state borders or cultural barriers – seem in retrospect merely secondary effects of that speed . . . [7]

In short, for some writers – referred to below as 'globalisation theorists' – globalisation has now become 'the central thematic for social theory',[8] and 'a key idea by which we understand the transition of human society into the third millennium'.[9]

The General Problem

On any sober intellectual reckoning, this is a curious outcome indeed. For the very idea of globalisation as an explanatory schema in its own right is fraught with difficulties. The term 'globalisation', after all, is at first sight merely a descriptive category, denoting either the geographical extension of social processes or possibly, as in Giddens' definition, 'the intensification of worldwide social relations'.[10] Now, since no-one denies that 'worldwide social relations' do indeed exist today in ways and to a degree that they never did before, there can be no objection to calls for a theory of globalisation, if that means an explanation of how and why these have come about. But such an explanation, if it is to avoid empty circularity, must fall back on some more basic social theory which could explain why the phenomena denoted by the term have become such a distinctive and salient feature of the contemporary world. (Globalisation as an outcome cannot be explained simply by invoking globalisation as a process tending towards that outcome.) Yet if that were so, and if, for example, time-space compression were to be explained as an emergent property of a particular historical type of social relations, then the term 'globalisation' would not denote a theory in its own right at all – instead it would function merely as a measure of how far and in what ways this historical process had developed. And the globalisation theorists clearly intend something more than this. By asserting that the emergence of a single global space as the arena of social action increasingly outweighs in its consequences other kinds of causality which have traditionally been invoked to explain social phenomena; by extrapolating the geographical dimension of this process into an alternative, spatio-temporal problematic for social science; and finally, by pitting this new problematic not simply against competing perspectives in the contemporary social sciences, but also against the classical foundations of modern social thought as a whole – in all these ways, they have raised their sights beyond any purely descriptive role for the concept. In the logical structure of their argumentation, what presents itself initially as the *explanandum* – globalisation as the developing outcome of some historical process – is progressively transformed into the *explanans*: it is globalisation which now explains the changing character of the modern world – and even generates 'retrospective discoveries' about past epochs in which it must be presumed not to have existed.

This inversion of *explanans* and *explanandum* cannot easily be rejected on purely logical grounds. After all, the consequences of a particular historical development may indeed go on to become significant causes in their own right, generating in turn further consequences which can no longer be derived from the original historical development. This is intrinsic to the nature of historical change. In this way, for example, Marx believed that the analysis of capitalist social relations had become fundamental to understanding modern societies, however much these relations were originally the product of other, necessarily pre-capitalist, causes. In fact, Marx also believed that the experience of capitalist society was an enabling condition of the intellectual formulation of the 'materialist conception of history', a new problematic, on the basis of which he too asserted the possibility of making 'retrospective discoveries' about the (pre-capitalist) past.[11] This comparison suggests that the claims of globalisation theory cannot simply be dismissed *a priori*. But it also alerts us to the real character of these claims. As Ankie Hoogvelt puts it, in one of the milder formulations which nonetheless captures nicely the kind of intellectual shift involved:

> [W]hat is being argued here is that, owing to the present reconstitution of the world into a single *social* space, that self-same historical process [which produced globalisation] has now lifted off and moved into a new ballpark. If, previously, global integration in the sense of a growing unification and interpenetration of the human condition was driven by the economic logic of capital accumulation, today it is the unification of the human condition that drives the logic of further capital accumulation.[12]

Within this shift we may identify the basic distinction which will be used in what follows, between a theory of globalisation and globalisation theory: the former might be constructed out of anything presumed to generate the spatio-temporal phenomena involved; the latter, by contrast, must derive its explanatory mechanism within those phenomena themselves: in short, it needs – even presupposes – a spatio-temporal reformulation of social theory itself. And it is this latter discourse of globalisation theory – an increasingly confident discourse within the literature – which will be interrogated in the pages which follow.

In order to appreciate what a curious development this is, it perhaps helps to remember that in the fields of sociology, anthropology, geography, historiography, philosophy and the history of ideas – to mention just a few – there have long existed rich literatures on the subject of space and time, some of them very extensive. The recognition that temporality and spatiality have varied across periods and cultures, that they have been socially constructed and mentally experienced in different ways, and that those different ways have themselves been highly consequential for the constitution of social orders – all this has been well and long established.[13]

Equally established, though remaining subject to important scholarly debates,[14] is the recognition that on any comparative review, the specifically modern, Western constructions of space and time which we might otherwise take for granted are thrown into sharp relief as historically exceptional, sociologically specific and culturally peculiar (in both senses of the word). The adjectives most commonly used to describe this peculiarity are 'abstracted', 'linear' and 'empty' or 'emptiable'. And, once again, considerable literatures have grown up around the attempt to understand when, how and where this particular construction of 'empty' space and time originated, the part which it played in the emergence and spread of 'modern' societies (from the Renaissance to the present, both in Europe and outside), and its crucial role (both sociological and philosophical) in both the organisation of social power and the construction of cultural meaning in those societies today.[15]

And yet, reading these literatures, one soon becomes aware – and this is surely the key point – that among the more serious contributions, *nobody* takes the word 'empty' literally. To be sure, they all recognise that at one level we can think of space and time as objectively contentless dimensions of existence within which human social (and other) processes are located and configured. Such processes can be analysed spatio-temporally – specifying how they mobilise the possibilities given 'objectively' as distance, proximity, duration, simultaneity, sequencing, and so on. And imagining space and time as empty, homogeneous, uniform and abstract is an intellectual precondition for conducting such forms of analysis. These writers also all recognise that the peculiarity of the modern, Western mobilisation of space and time does indeed lie precisely in the fact that it uniquely posits this 'empty', 'scientific' conception as the central form of its own cultural and social construction of space and time – and that this in turn is a constitutive condition of many important dimensions of modern social reproduction: bureaucratic organisation, historicist forms of consciousness, bordered nation-states, and so on.[16]

But there it ends. For the kind of questions first applied to other periods and cultures in order to understand why it should be that the Nuer, the Tiv, the Algerian peasant, the Maya, the ancient Greek, the

Balinese, the Chinese, and so on, have lived in such different spatio-temporal worlds from the modern European must equally be formulated for modernity itself. The apparent correspondence of ideas of empty space and time to the properties of a pre-social natural universe does not change the fact that those ideas too are 'full' of social and cultural determinations. It only makes those determinations easier to miss, and therefore more prone to naturalisation.

The simple way of avoiding that outcome is to insert the following question at the base of the analysis: in what kind of society (or culture) do the spatio-temporal dimensions of existence take on the historically peculiar forms of 'emptiable' space and time – and why? It is the methodological priority of this question which implicitly governs the logical structure of, for example, Robert David Sack's treatment of space in *Human Territoriality: Its Theory and History*, or Donald Lowe's analysis of temporality in *A History of Bourgeois Perception* – or indeed Nicos Poulantzas' extraordinary analysis of what he called 'the underlying conceptual matrices of space and time'.[17] And far from minimising subsequent questions about the importance of space and time in the constitution of social reality, it is rather what enables them to be framed as properly sociological questions in the first place.

Thus, even (or above all) in the specialised study of space and time, where spatio-temporal phenomena loom largest, the move to reverse the normal relation of *explanans* and *explanandum* – to make space and time themselves into the fundamental basis of explanation – is generally resisted. Instead the characteristic first move is rather the sociological and phenomenological deconstruction of the emptiness of modern space and time, by reference to the specific social and cultural relations which produce and reproduce them in this form. In this way, the emergence of a spatio-temporal problematic *per se* is effectively ruled out. And one can readily understand why. Whatever Newtonian or post-Newtonian physics might tell us about the natural world, no human ever experiences spatial or temporal determinants which are not mediated or constructed in particular socio-cultural forms.

Attempts, therefore, to construct a general nomenclature of spatio-temporal analysis may indeed be highly illuminating in the service of comparative analysis – enabling us to see how different social worlds differently produce the common parameters of distance and proximity, duration, simultaneity and sequence, and so on. However, if these categories are inserted too deeply into the logical structure of social explanation, they must lead to arguments which, as Sack diplomatically puts it, 'over-generalise about the significance of space'.[18] And there is a further danger, inherent in this over-generalising: that the properties of 'empty' space and time (which in fact derive from the social and cultural determinants of these modern forms) will be unwittingly attributed to the 'objective' character of space and time themselves – naturalising and thus rendering indecipherable the very phenomena whose effects have prompted the theoretical inflation of space and time in the first place. They will, in short, be reified. In this quite elemental theoretical mistake, it will be argued below, we can find both the ultimate source and the unavoidable destination of globalisation theory. This is its general problem.

'Nature in you', says Regan, addressing her increasingly deranged father,

> . . . stands on the very verge
> Of her confine: you should be rul'd and led
> By some discretion that discerns your state
> Better than you yourself.[19]

The contemporary social sciences, it seems, in their aspiration to a spatio-temporal problematic, stand on the very verge of their possibility of coherence. In globalisation theory, we shall try to show, they overstep that verge.

In this book three separate instances of that overstepping will be analysed – in the works successively of Jan Aart Scholte, Rob Walker and Anthony Giddens. The first of these is a writer who embraces globalisation theory in the field of International Relations (IR); the second straddles the boundary between IR and political philosophy;

the last occupies the field of 'straight' social theory, and is surely globalisation theory's most eminent sociological exponent. By
counterposing these three examples, each coming from a different
intellectual direction (and none of the texts significantly cross-refer-
encing either of the others), we can draw out the common fallacy
which lies within the ambition of globalisation theory.

But the purpose is by no means entirely negative. Globalisation
theory, for all its intellectual tribulations, has this virtue: it throws into
new relief two things which are worth debating and defending. The
first of these is the status of classical social theory – represented in
these pages above all by Karl Marx and, secondarily, Max Weber – in
the continuing enterprise of social science. Since this enterprise itself
has meaning only in relation to an evolving historical reality, the question of whether and how far ideas developed in the nineteenth and
early twentieth century can still retain their relevance to the contemporary world is entirely legitimate. More, it is this questioning which
compels adherents of what C. Wright Mills called the tradition of
Classic Social Analysis[20] to refresh and extend that tradition by trying
to demonstrate how its methods and insights can illuminate an historical reality which might indeed seem to have moved decisively
beyond their analytical reach. In this book that positive goal necessarily takes on a negative form: the critique of other writers. Yet
hopefully, in the course of the critique, the value of what is being
defended will also become more clear. However, if strong judgements
are made about these other writers, that should not be read as an
attempt to delegitimise their work. For the truth of the matter is that
the present writer is indebted to them for stimulating him to draw out
his own arguments the more carefully. The strongest of our disagree-
ments remain therefore in the end subordinate to what surely unites
us: the common pursuit of a collective effort to understand the social
world.

The second issue which is thrown into new relief by the debate
over globalisation is the idea of 'the international' as a significant and
distinctive dimension of the social world of modernity. The sometimes

rather extreme dismissal of this by globalisation theory forces us to take stock of the notion, and to clarify what, if anything, should be preserved within it. What is at stake here?

'International Relations' and Globalisation Theory

If 'the divisions of the continents and of the globe as a whole' are indeed breaking down, and if the claims of globalisation theory are the legitimate theoretical implication of this, then it is not only the notion of 'society' as a territorially bounded entity which must give way to the emergent reality. International theory too – traditionally defined as the study of interactions across, between and among such entities – must also be subjected to fundamental modification. Thus Jan Aart Scholte holds that a 'methodological territorialism' is written into the very definition of 'inter-national' relations. This, he argues, blinds academics and policy-makers alike to the 'supra-territorial' character of contemporary global challenges. For these are increasingly constituted not in the territorial space of the 'Westphalian states-system' but rather in that 'distanceless space' promoted by modern financial markets, satellite communications and computer networks. Urgent intellectual rectification is now required: 'it is arguably dangerous to give methodological territorialism further lease on life in a globalising world.'[21]

The rectification of international theory has not proceeded as far or as fast as globalisation theorists in other disciplines would advocate. According to Malcolm Waters, international theory has proved unable so far to move beyond 'a proto-theory of globalization'[22] in which attention to processes of transnational integration co-exist problematically with claims for the continuing significance of the sovereign state: this 'dualism remains the bottom line for political science and international relations versions of globalization'.[23] Yet if the battle for globalisation theory has not yet been won in this field, still the tocsin has sounded. And a proliferation of books and articles has indeed

appeared in recent years taking up the new nomenclature and pro-
claiming the end of the 'Westphalian System'.[24] In varying degrees and
with differing nuances, these writings have claimed that the organisation of the world by and around a system of sovereign, territorial
nation-states is gradually submerging beneath new kinds of (non-territorial) linkages. The intensification of these linkages is in turn
producing a new spatial and institutional configuration of social
power – a 'postinternational' system[25] – whose shape corresponds less
and less to the interstate model provided by orthodox International
Relations.

In the discussion which follows below, two lines will be drawn in the
sand concerning this matter. First, it will be argued that the prior existence of a 'Westphalian System', which serves as the crucial historical
foil for the theoretical significance of contemporary claims about globalisation, is actually quite mythical. Defining the modern international
system purely in terms of geopolitical norms of interaction between
states, it derives in fact from the (sociologically) narrowest of international theories – political realism. And it has always stood in the way of
a much richer understanding of the international derived from analysis of the wider historical process of capitalist world development – a
process rendered invisible, or at any rate irrelevant, by the notion of a
Westphalian System. Exactly why globalisation theory – that most for-
ward-looking of doctrines – should have made itself intellectually
dependent on this most traditionalist of historical premises will be
examined towards the end of chapter 2.

Yet if the first line to be drawn points to a critique of the discipline
of International Relations, the second, perhaps surprisingly, will cross
over the first to mount an equally emphatic defence. For the merging
in globalisation theory of the idea of 'the international' with the belief
in a (now fading) Westphalian System passes all too easily into an outright denial of any remaining analytical determinacy to those general
questions which are raised – in different ways in different historical
epochs – by interrelations across, between and among human societies. It passes, that is, into the rejection of what might be called 'the

problematic of the international', which is conventionally taken to compose the distinctive subject matter of international theory. This is a rejection endorsed, in his own complicated way, by Rob Walker in his book *Inside/Outside: International Relations as Political Theory.*[26] And we shall therefore, in chapter 3, use that work as a limit case for this argument, attempting to construct in critical counterpoint a defensible version of that 'problematic of the international'.

International Relations, International Relations: why should anyone care about the academic discipline of International Relations? And why should any readers located outside its parochial and possibly superannuated disciplinary confines take any interest at all in such an arcane procedure as the one just proposed? The answer is that they may not be as far outside it as they think. In fact, they may not be outside it at all.

For we live today in a veritable 'age of globalisation studies', in which one academic discipline after another is gaily expanding its remit into the 'global' sphere and relocating its own subject matter in a geographically extended, worldwide perspective. This extension leads these other disciplines onto the intellectual terrain of IR, for which the existence of an increasingly worldwide 'international system' has always necessarily constituted the empirical object of study. The arrival of all these newcomers cannot fail to bring welcome enrichment to a field which, especially during the Cold War, often seemed condemned to a permanent intellectual poverty. At the same time, the question of whether the pre-existing incumbents had, for all their faults, identified anything of real significance actually matters a great deal for the newcomers themselves. If they had not – or if what they identified turned out to have been a purely local historical phenomenon (such as the Westphalian System), which they had never properly understood, and whose conditions were in any case now passing – then of course they can safely be ignored.

But a word of friendly advice: the newcomers should be careful. For if, on the other hand, the accumulated reflections of past international theorists were in fact clustered around intellectual problems of more general and enduring significance, then a quite different prognosis must be entertained for any newcomers unwary enough to discount this possibility. Either they will find themselves repeating the exercise of generations of liberal and other 'idealists' in this discipline, whose interventions against the realist orthodoxy have foundered on their inability to suppress the significance of these general problems. Or they will engage in a laborious process of unwittingly reinventing the problematic of the international itself under a different name. Zygmunt Bauman is surely not alone in suffering this latter fate, but his example remains nonetheless a spectacular one:

> The problem is . . . that sociology so far is poorly equipped to treat the social space beyond the confines of the nation-state as anything else but the analytically compressed 'environment'.
>
> It is only now that we begin to understand to what extent all major categories of sociology are dependent for their meaning and practical usefulness on their relatedness to the typically inner-societal space, different from all other imaginable social spaces by being *held together by a universally* (i.e. within that space) *binding authority*. . . . I suggest that the elaboration of categories appropriate to the analysis of dependencies and interactions in the 'non-societal' social space, a space without 'principal coordination', 'dominant culture', 'legitimate authority', etc., is now a most urgent task faced by sociology. . . . the reality to be modelled is, both in its present shape and in its plausible prospects, much more fluid, heterogeneous and 'under-patterned' than anything the sociologists have tried to grasp intellectually in the past.[27]

What Bauman 'only now . . . begin[s] to understand' has of course been the central, defining assertion of the orthodox study of IR for generations.

Thus to those coming from outside, for whom the theme of globalisation may well have offered a valuable means of transcending disciplinary boundaries elsewhere, and who therefore wonder why the discipline of IR looms so large in chapters 2 and 3, the answer must be that the old adage may still apply: *de te fabula narratur.*[28]

That said, however, the fundamental problem with globalisation theory lies not in the difficulties of its encounter with International Relations, but rather in the deeper contradiction already alluded to at the level of social theory itself: the attempt to construct 'globalisation' as an *explanans* leads to a conceptual inflation of 'the spatial' which is both difficult to justify ontologically and liable to produce not explanations but reifications. And yet we have also said that this charge is impossible to substantiate *a priori*. How, then, should we proceed? The answer can only be that we must examine the outcome of these assumptions in the texts of the globalisation theorists themselves. Is it really true that globalisation theory makes its adherents dependent on such large theoretical claims about the significance of space? If so, how do they seek to ground those claims? And in any case, do these claims, in turn, really lie at the heart of the explanatory difficulties which they experience? We have to look and see.

If any one of the three key assertions we are making – the necessity to globalisation theory of the conceptual inflation of space, the impossibility of its grounding in an alternative problematic for social theory, the inevitability of its reificatory consequences for concrete explanations – is contradicted by the evidence we find, then our overall intellectual case against globalisation theory will fail.

If, on the other hand, they are all confirmed, then we may perhaps make the following prediction. The more vigorously and systematically the case for globalisation as an *explanans* is pursued, the more explicitly and disruptively those inherent problems will manifest themselves. In the end, the intellectual cost of this will prove so high that one of two outcomes must result. Either the claims of globalisation theory will be *tacitly* withdrawn (after successive attempts at substantiation have failed), within the very process of the argumentation itself. This, we shall attempt to show in some detail, is what happens in Giddens' *Consequences of Modernity*. Alternatively, those claims will be from the start the object of such powerful intellectual equivocations that the authors will prevent themselves, perhaps wisely, from allowing them free rein. The consequence of this latter policy, however, strongly illustrated in the case of Jan Aart Scholte, is that no clear, definitive argument can be permitted to emerge at all. Prevented from reaching their full height, yet asserted nonetheless in some necessarily tumble-down form, these claims will come to resemble instead the intellectual equivalent of an architectural folly.

Yet if globalisation theory necessarily has this self-confounding quality, why take the trouble to subject it to a scholarly critique? Why not simply wait for it to collapse of its own accord? The answer is twofold. First, our suspicions and predictions remain at this stage only suspicions and predictions. They have yet to be substantiated. And second, the current fashionability of globalisation theory has not come without a price. For arguably the claims which it makes, if taken seriously, combine to exercise a kind of theoretical veto over other, more valuable resources for understanding both the contemporary world in general and its international politics in particular. Before we move on to the next chapter, we should therefore pause to spell out what this veto comprises.

It seems to have three main elements. First, insofar as it represents the contemporary world as having moved decisively beyond the imaginative reach of classical writers such as Karl Marx and Max Weber, globalisation theory in fact jettisons a vital resource for understanding exactly the spatio-temporal phenomena which it deems so significant. Once cut off from the rich explanatory schemas of classical social theory, these phenomena are instead converted into irreducible causes in their own right – unavoidably renaturalising the very things which it was the achievement of those earlier writers to problematise and demystify. A central feature of this process is the systematic fetishising of spatial categories, a possibility latent in the term 'globalisation' itself, but fully activated only by the role which it is now called upon to play in the construction of social explanation. This in turn produces a paradoxical *reduction* in the explanatory claims of social science. For the deepest level of the classical interrogation of modernity – the one at which its most dramatic and counter-intuitive discoveries were made – is now increasingly sealed off anew by the progressive rehabilitation of old reifications in a new technical language.

Second, by conflating the general intellectual issue of relations between societies with a specific historical form of those relations, caricatured as 'the Westphalian System', globalisation theory mistakes a subsequent evolution in that form for the obsolescence of the problematic of the international itself. In this respect, far from achieving an advance on existing international theory, it simply abandons the field, and haplessly reproduces many of the fallacies of liberal idealism – thereby joining the latter in the particular ideological division of labour through which the realist orthodoxy has for so long secured its place. The 'realist' response, when it comes, will presumably be as devastating for globalisation theory as it has always been for alternative approaches which have left untheorised the terrain of geopolitics where the intellectual counter-attack traditionally mobilises.

Finally, by embodying nonetheless the dominant site of convergence today between sociological thought and International Relations, globalisation theory constitutes the latest, and in some ways the most disruptive, obstacle to the great desideratum of this field: a genuinely social theory of the international system. And that, as already suggested, is no longer (if it ever was) a matter of concern to international theorists alone. Despite its origins in sociology and its attention to international processes, globalisation theory thus does neither credit to the one nor justice to the other.

Any one of these problems on its own would tell against the wisdom of embracing such an approach as 'the central thematic for social theory'. In combination, however, and when added to the obfuscatory role which the term plays in public debate, they surely warrant a more active and critical diagnosis. And that is what this book seeks to provide.

2

Scholte's Folly

Introduction

'I hope that the pursuit of foolhardy ambitions has nevertheless yielded a provocative argument.' So writes Jan Aart Scholte in the Preface to *Globalization: A Critical Introduction*.[1] Scholte is anything but foolhardy. Although we shall certainly suggest that his understanding of 'supraterritoriality' is highly problematic, we shall also see that it has the real intellectual merit of trying to pin down an argument about globalisation in a clear and precise way. More to the point, Scholte is in some respects the most sober of globalisation theorists. He asserts no instant, overall transformation of everything, but draws attention instead to the 'intricate interplay' between the new forces of globalisation and the persistence nonetheless of the old world which they may or may not be in the process of transforming. Vast quantities of data are assembled to document the reality of these forces – yet equally telling statistics are also presented which undercut their significance. Theoretical claims which might elsewhere be built up into far-reaching arguments are here deliberately prevented from rising to their full height. Thus, 'globalization has rendered methodological territorialism obsolete . . . and . . . requires us substantially to rethink social theory'. And yet this same globalisation 'has thus far shown few signs of bringing an end to the predominance of capitalism in production, bureaucratism in governance, communitarianism in community, and rationalism in knowledge'.[2] Rarely does one see such bold theoretical arguments being subjected to such sweeping empirical qualification by their own author in the very process of their formulation.

And it is to this particular feature of his work that the title of this chapter in fact alludes. For like the 'follies' of those nineteenth-century enthusiasts whose architectural fancies still decorate the countryside, Scholte's argument about globalisation is somehow necessarily built as a ruin. At any rate, his better judgement seems again and again to tell him that the walls, whatever their occasional altitude, must be left incomplete; the flagstones, to prevent misunderstanding, should be laid cracked and irregular. Even the tower of definition, which supports the other parts of the argument and lends the whole its distinctive form, partakes of the general tumbledown effect.

To view this folly in all its craggy magnificence, one need only turn to pages eight and nine of the book where the argument is laid out helpfully in the tabular form of eight propositions and six sub-propositions. 'Buts', 'althoughs' and other qualificatory signals mark the points at which the structure has been deliberately left open to the elements. Thus, globalisation *is* a 'transformation', *but* one which augments rather than displaces pre-existing social phenomena. It has come into its own 'since the 1960s' – *although* it 'made earlier appearances' before that. Today it appears unstoppable, *but* it need not go on that way, *though* the chances of it slowing down 'seem remote at present'. And so on. Clearly, this is a labour not of foolhardiness, but rather of meticulous care.

Aesthetic convention allows that an architectural folly, well executed, can achieve a real artistic integrity in its deliberate incompleteness. But does the same hold intellectually? Can an intellectual argument be built in the same way and escape judgement? Can the arguments for globalisation theory consistently be built in any other way? These are the questions which we must address to Scholte's folly.

And what we shall find is as follows. First, it is indeed necessary for the very definition of globalisation to manifest these folly-like characteristics. For unless that definition can identify something not already explained by other concepts, it can make no contribution of its own to the work of the social sciences. And yet the more it is driven, in pursuit of this, to differentiate itself analytically and refine itself into a purely spatial category, the smaller the empirical remit becomes of what it can claim to explain at all. And there appears to be no way out of this problem – for it is rooted in the prior conceptual inflation of space which is intrinsic to globalisation theory itself.

This definitional dilemma, however, is as nothing compared with the enormity and implausibility of the *historical* assumptions which become necessary if the impact of globalisation is to be represented on the scale desired by its advocates. In order for the contemporary proliferation of transnational relations to acquire decisive historical significance, it must be believed that their 'transborder' character transgresses some basic ordering principle of the international system as it previously existed. And this need, secondly, and paradoxically, leads the globalisation theorists to endorse as their own model of the past the traditional realist idea of the Westphalian System. That model indeed portrays a world of sovereign political units, asserting absolute, inviolable jurisdiction over bordered territorial spaces. Compared with that model, the transborder flows identified by globalisation theory do indeed look revolutionary, and their significance does seem to rest on their reflection of a specifically spatial development – which Scholte will call the rise of supraterritorial space.

Yet even here, the folly must re-assert itself, for there is a problem. The period in which these 'Westphalian' conditions are held to have obtained runs apparently from the mid-seventeenth century to the mid-twentieth century. It is therefore bisected by the emergence in England of industrial capitalism at the end of the eighteenth century. And that event had two consequences which condemn the historical definition of globalisation to the same endless equivocations which we shall see attending its analytical definition. On the one hand, it led, as we shall see, to a proliferation of highly significant supraterritorial relations – at the very chronological centre of the supposedly territorial Westphalian Era. And on the other hand, it was also associated with a transformation in the nature of politics, as a result of which these supraterritorial relations could and did go on expanding without, however, contradicting the territoriality of sovereignty at all (however much they might at times have complicated the exercise of political power).

Neither of these two consequences is visible to the Westphalian model, which implies instead a continuity of territorially defined geopolitics across the period as a whole. Yet each has empirical implications which unavoidably complicate the claims of globalisation theory. The eruption of supraterritorial relations in a period where they were supposed not to exist compels Scholte to acknowledge that the forces of globalisation which have so transformed the world 'since the 1960s' somehow 'made earlier appearances' *inside* the very Westphalian System whose *negation* they would later be interpreted as representing. Meanwhile, the corresponding transformation of the nature of sovereignty – described by Marx as 'the abstraction of the political state' – arguably stands behind what Scholte can only report as an inexplicable empirical outcome: namely, that even present-day globalisation mysteriously fails to deliver the truly epochal effects which, viewed through the lens of Westphalia, it seems so obviously to entail.

Several times in his book, Scholte credits Marx with being 'prescient' for 'anticipating' the rise of globalisation. Marx, however, hardly needed to be prescient. The social relations which actually constitute the phenomena which so impress the globalisation theorists were already at work in the industrial revolution in England. And by the 1850s at the latest, Marx had forged a sociological explanation for them which, applied to the international system today, would render the follies of globalisation theory unnecessary.

A Definitional Achievement

We remarked in the Introduction to this volume that in order for the concept of globalisation to begin its work as an *explanans*, two principal conditions must be fulfilled. On the one hand, in order to grasp anything determinate at all, the concept must be defined in a non-circular manner, avoiding such formulations as 'globalization is the present process of becoming global'.[3] On the other hand, in order to prevent the concept reverting immediately to an *explanandum*, the phenomenon which it is claimed to grasp must be a feature of reality not already explained by other, pre-existing concepts. And we further speculated that, given the spatial resonance of the term, globalisation theory would end by seeking its explanatory mechanism in specifically spatial phenomena. Finally, we noted that this in turn would logically require (though not necessarily receive) an underlying justification for the resultant, sudden elevation of space as a starting point for social explanation.

This is indeed the logical sequence followed by Scholte. And it leads to exactly the outcome just described. Recognising the need to clarify a very confused debate, he starts by rejecting circular definitions such as the one cited above, and then moves immediately on to provide a list of five possible meanings for the word 'globalisation': internationalisation, liberalisation, universalisation, Westernisation/ modernisation and deterritorialisation.[4] 'Globalisation' has been used, he says, to describe each and all of these phenomena. Yet many of them are phenomena of long standing, which therefore do not warrant the introduction of a new term. More importantly, if globalisation were simply, say, liberalisation, then it would already have been explained as an effect of 'free' trade. (It would be an *explanandum.*) For this reason, and in short order, each of the first four possible meanings is declared 'redundant' as the basis of an adequate definition. Only the last – 'deterritorialization' – can provide that basis. For, according to Scholte, it alone identifies something which is historically new, which has a real causal significance that is irreducible to the others, and which therefore merits the use of a new term.

The argumentation has been a little shaky at certain points. The assumption that the concept *must* after all have a real world object to justify its explanatory status leans quite heavily at this stage on an argument from linguistic usage: 'when new vocabulary gains currency, it is often because it captures an important change that is taking place in the world.'[5] True enough, although the same argument is later prevented from lending any equivalent support to the concept of sovereignty: 'persistent rhetoric of sovereignty is quite different from continued viability of sovereignty.'[6] But never mind. We have arrived at first base: having delineated by a process of elimination the significant content of the term, a preliminary definition is now available: 'globalization refers to a far-reaching change in the nature of social space.'[7]

Now, in order for such a claim to acquire real explanatory power, the significance of space must next be raised to (or rediscovered at) a higher level in the apparatus of social explanation more generally. Only then would it follow that 'a far-reaching change' in the nature of space would necessarily have correspondingly 'far-reaching significance' for social reproduction as a whole. Once again, Scholte has understood this, for his next move is indeed an attempt to consolidate that wider claim about the role of space. How then does he proceed?

At this point it pays to remember that the building under construction here is a folly. Nothing else can explain the strange manner in which the very cornerstones of the argument are about to be laid. On the one hand, some kind of claim must now be made to support the argument which is to follow. On the other hand, Scholte is too cautious to grant the outright analytical priority to space which globalisation theory really needs. Thus, in the seven-sentence paragraph on page forty-six where the general case for space is asserted, bold assertion and heavy qualification alternate with each other, almost on a sentence-by-sentence basis. Space is 'a core determinant of social life' – a status which, however, it shares with a series of other 'primary dimensions' which include 'culture, economy, politics and psychology'. With all of these, indeed, it is 'on a par'. Spatial phenomena 'strongly influence' these other dimensions – and yet the same applies 'vice versa'. Halfway through the paragraph we seem to be headed for a straight geographical determinism, in which 'differences between the lives of desert nomads, mountain villagers and island seafarers are largely attributable to contrasts in the places they inhabit.' This, however, is immediately qualified by a re-assertion of the 'mutually constitutive' relationship between geographical and other 'primary dimensions'. The final sentence is then left to render what positive account it can from the preceding transactions: 'If the character of a society's map changes, then its culture, ecology, economics, politics and social psychology are likely to shift as well.'

As cornerstones go, this is not a premise that looks likely to carry the weight of any particularly heavy explanatory claims. Fortunately, it will not have to. For he has already told us, with appropriate caution, that globalisation, however far-reaching its significance, has in fact *not* yielded any 'deeper transformations' of the other primary dimensions of social life.[8] Thus guarded, it is therefore a perfectly reasonable statement. Where then does he take the argument next?

Leaving behind the question of the general significance of space, Scholte now offers to specify exactly what this change is in 'the nature of social space' which globalisation comprises. In a nutshell, globalisation has brought about the end of 'territorialism'. Territorialism refers to a social geography in which all the relationships through which people are interconnected can be 'mapped on the earth's surface and measured on a three-dimensional grid of longitude, latitude and altitude'.[9] Under such conditions, there are no 'places' whose location cannot be identified on this grid (even if they are not stationary); every location is separated from every other location by an absolute distance (however minute its extent or the time required to cross it); and every tract of space can be separated off from those around it by a single line. Territorialism, indeed, 'implies that macro social space is wholly organized' in terms of spatial units governed by these three territorial laws of position, distance and separation – with the further consequence that any relations among or across these units, governed as they must be by the same laws, are therefore properly described as 'interterritorial'. 'Until recently,' Scholte says, in a sudden, breathtaking reconnection of these observations with world history, 'social geography across the world had a territorialist character.' At this point, then, the possibility of dramatic explanatory significance, wavering uncertainly during the earlier general discussion of space, returns with a vengeance. This portion of the folly has been built up to its full height.

And we soon learn why. For using this construction, Scholte is now able to produce a definition of 'global' phenomena and relationships which is of quite unexampled precision. He invites us to consider the phenomena of 'telephone calls, electronic finance and the depletion of the stratospheric ozone'. The first two of these make the really significant point because they are media of social interaction. And the point is this: all previous surges of 'time-space compression' reduced (via accelerated communication) the impact of the laws of location, distance and separation without finally overturning them. But for telephone or computer communications, territorial distance is not simply of reduced significance: it is effectively of no significance at all. They are therefore 'supraterritorial'. And the '[t]ransworld simultaneity'[10] which they unprecedentedly allow means that (some) social relations can now operate outside the laws of territorial space. Following Manuel Castells, Scholte argues that a new 'space of flows' now opens out alongside the old 'space of places'.

Still, why call these supraterritorial interactions 'global'? The remarkable answer is that the term 'global' will now be used to mark a precise limit, rather than referring, as it so often does, to an indefinite expansiveness. The technologies which achieve effective simultaneity for social relations on planet Earth would be unable to do the same beyond it. 'Time again becomes a significant factor in respect of radio signals when they have to cover interplanetary and longer distances.' Thus 'global' relations are those which, strictly within the planetary space of the globe and its orbiting communications satellites, are no longer subject to the laws of position, distance and separation. And these, says Scholte, are historically unprecedented: 'New terminology is unavoidable.'

One has to admire the definitional achievement here. Scholte has taken one of the woolliest terms in current academic and other parlance, and he has specified for it a content of surely unbeatable exactitude. In fact, it is so exact that Scholte himself will be forced to loosen it almost immediately in order to avoid the extreme technological determinism which it would otherwise prescribe. Still, it is ingenious nonetheless. And enormous interest must now attach to the question of which social relations have taken on these new properties, and with what effect.

Before embarking on his survey of global activities, Scholte reiterates the precision he has laboured so hard to establish. Globalisation, understood as the rise of supraterritoriality, 'is *not* the same thing as internationalization, liberalization, universalization or modernization'.[11] Indeed, 'almost invariably', scepticism about globalisation derives precisely from the failure to distinguish it from these four other phenomena.

The reader is therefore in for a shock. For as the survey of global activities gets underway, the same definition which had appeared, in its formulation, to be demanding in the extreme turns out, in its application, to be possessed of a veritable Midas touch.[12] All manner of things now start to gleam with the appearance of 'globality' – nuclear missiles, confederations of trades unions, even the *Teletubbies* children's programme. Jet aeroplanes somehow make it onto the roster of 'supraterritorial connections'. '[T]ens of thousands' of multinational corporations turn out to have been 'imprecisely named' – they are 'global companies'. Their productive activities somehow count as 'supraterritorial' even though all that appears to be at work is the outweighing of one territorial consideration – costs of transport and cross-border movement – by another: '[d]ifferences in local [*sic*] costs of labour, regulation and taxation'. International organisations (such as the United Nations, the International Monetary Fund, the World Trade Organisation, and so on) are now 'global organisations' because they 'extend across the planet'. (Only a page earlier, this characteristic would have qualified them as 'universal', but emphatically not as 'global': 'Universality says something about territorial extent, whereas globality says something about space-time relations'.) A multinational bank syndicate lending US dollars to a borrower in the Dominican Republic is in fact making a 'global bank loan' in a 'global currency'. And this is despite the fact that money (of all things) would now struggle to meet the earlier definition of 'supraterritoriality'. For the strongest claim Scholte is now prepared to make for money is that it 'has become considerably (though of course not completely) detached from territorial space'. Indeed, so capacious does the argument now become that it will admit anything which can show 'an at least partly global character'. And sundry forms of environmental problem make it into this category on the grounds that 'none of them can be territorially contained'.

Thus, one by one, the four additional meanings of globalisation, earlier discarded as 'redundant', are now allowed back into the concept. And one can understand why. After all, just how many phenomena – apart from telecommunications – could really satisfy that earlier definition in all its rigour? And even for those telecommunications, how much causality could really be squeezed out of the simple fact of their 'globality' – without reference, that is, to the (non-spatially defined) social character of the activities themselves which human beings were using these new media to pursue? And what would then become of the overall claim that globalisation itself, defined strictly as deterritorialisation, is of 'far-reaching' real-world significance? Analytical precision or real empirical weight – that was the choice that had to be made. And with 267 pages of the book still to go, who could blame any author for choosing empirical weight? This portion of the building, central as it is, must definitely be left open to the elements.

Yet what determinate claims *can* be made for globalisation, now that its meaning has loosened again? And how are they to be framed? The answer is that large historical claims are nonetheless about to be made. And they will be framed above all with implicit reference to the subject matter and the intellectual procedures of the academic discipline of International Relations.

When Was the Westphalian System?

The subject matter of International Relations, as we have earlier noted, is an unavoidable destination for globalisation theory: for this discipline necessarily takes the world system as a whole for its object of empirical and theoretical investigation. How successfully it has discharged this distinctive vocation is debatable. The point is simply that it lies in the path of globalisation theory, and the latter cannot help bouncing off it at some point. In Scholte's case, the encounter is generally more implicit than explicit, perhaps because he is part of a (not inconsiderable) traffic moving in the other direction. 'As a sign of these times,' he says, 'I started this book while attached to an International Relations faculty and completed it in a Centre for the Study of Globalisation and Regionalisation.'[13] The encounter is there nonetheless. What form does it take?

In an earlier published version of this chapter, the theoretical engagement with IR was more explicit. There Scholte argued openly that globalisation 'calls into question the adequacy' of both IR and comparative politics as forms of social analysis. Territorialist assumptions were, he suggested, '[i]nherent in the concept of "inter-national"'. And the impact of globalisation gave 'ample cause for a paradigm shift in social analysis' towards what he called a 'world system methodology'. By this Scholte did not mean an embrace of the World Systems Theory approach associated with Immanuel Wallerstein – an approach which he charged with having 'supplanted one type of territorialism with another'. Rather he meant that analysis should proceed by conceiving reality as an 'interrelation of spaces', themselves seen as 'interconnected dimensions of "world" space', but with no assumption made in advance about the analytical priority of 'any particular spatial framework'. And in this context, dropping the word 'international' in favour of '"world" would reflect a full-scale methodological reorientation'.[14]

In the book version, references to the discipline of IR have mostly been removed. However, the historical claims about the nature of the international itself have been preserved almost untouched. And in line with just about every other critical engagement of globalisation theory with IR, they centre on that great bugbear of international theory: the Westphalian System.

The Peace of Westphalia in 1648 marked the formal end of the Thirty Years War, and with it the end too of the wars of religion which followed the Protestant Reformation.[15] By asserting the prerogatives of the German princes against the Holy Roman Emperor, and of secular rulers in general against the interference of the Catholic Church, it registered a heavy decline of the hierarchical and 'transnational' principles which had been central to the medieval geopolitical organisation of Christendom. And it held its place as the major overall legal codification and territorial settlement of European geopolitics for the century and a half leading up to the wars of the French Revolution and the Congress of Vienna in 1815.

For international theory, however (and to some extent in the fields of international law and political theory too),[16] its iconic significance extends far beyond any historical term in which its detailed and highly complicated legal and territorial provisions might have continued to apply.[17] Looking back from the twentieth-century world of bordered, sovereign states, Westphalia appears instead as a turning point in world history: the point at which sovereignty (however embryonically conceived or unevenly implemented) began visibly to be consolidated as the organisational principle of a European states-system which would later expand across the planet. Viewed in this light, the Peace of Westphalia reappears as the originary dispensation of geopolitical modernity itself. And the present-day international system, composed as it still legally is of sovereign, independent states, is therefore often referred to as 'the Westphalian System'.

This nomenclature has been sharply contested – both by those who argue that medieval practices lived on after and in spite of Westphalia, and by those who argue that its early modern conception of sovereignty differs fundamentally from the later, capitalist form which characterises the world of today.[18] By contrast, some of the strongest attachments in IR theory to this idea of a Westphalian System have been formed, on the one hand, by 'traditional' thinkers (for whom sovereignty in the broadest sense of 'constitutional separateness' remains the most significant fact about international relations) and, on the other hand . . . by globalisation theorists.

For example, in an article entitled 'Globalization and the End of the Old Order', David Held and Anthony McGrew identify the cross-cutting, overlapping territorialities of globalisation as 'a unique challenge to a world order designed in accordance with the Westphalian principle of sovereign, exclusive rule over a bounded territory'. They claim that this challenge is already promoting 'the emergence of a post-Westphalian world order'. And (in a formulation which expresses just how much of the international itself they believe would change with the passing of its Westphalian form) they assert their conviction that 'through a process of progressive, incremental change, geo-political forces will come to be socialized into democratic agencies and practices.'[19] In *Global Transformations*, Held and his co-authors go on to set out in seven-point detail the 'model of Westphalia' which will serve as the benchmark against which the transformations wrought by globalisation are to be measured.[20] And they do this in the belief not that the historical Peace of Westphalia itself definitively established these norms of geopolitical regulation, but rather that what is conventionally called 'the Westphalian System' did in fact govern the nature of international relations until the new forces of globalisation began their work of dramatic transformation.

And so it is with Scholte too. Although the 'folly' will not extend with quite such confidence into the future, he appears to buy fully into the same historical assumptions which Held et al., in the company of 'traditional' IR theory, are willing to concede about the past. 'After all,' he says, 'the Westphalian states-system that arose in the seventeenth century and spread worldwide by the middle of the twentieth century was quintessentially territorial.'[21] So much so, in fact, that so long as the Westphalian System obtained, 'methodological territorialism' itself, the greatest obstacle to understanding the world today, 'offered a broadly viable intellectual shortcut' for social inquiry. The point is rounded out into the wider argument about knowledge and society which it entails – and which links up in turn with the claims made earlier for the significance of linguistic usage. Pre-Westphalian thought was non-territorialist because social life was not organised territorially; consequently, 'no scholarly research [sic] undertaken a thousand years ago made reference to bounded territorial spaces.' During the Westphalian era, methodological territorialism was intellectually reasonable because it genuinely 'reflected the social conditions of a particular epoch'. It is only now, after the erosion of these conditions by globalisation during the second half of the twentieth century, that it becomes necessary for us 'to develop an alternative, nonterritorialist cartography of social life'.

Yet is this really plausible? The notion that there existed, up until the mid-twentieth century, an international system which was 'quintessentially territorial' is a very debatable one indeed – and that on both empirical and theoretical grounds.

Consider, for example, Gallagher and Robinson's famous article of 1953, 'The Imperialism of Free Trade'.[22] The entire force of their argument there was devoted to explaining why the British Empire, from at least the early nineteenth century onwards, could not even be fully seen, let alone understood, using what Scholte defines as a territorialist method. '[I]t would clearly be unreal', they wrote, 'to define imperial history exclusively as the history of those colonies coloured red on the map.' Such a procedure would be equivalent to 'judging the size and character of icebergs solely from the parts above the water-line'. For already, they claimed, a new kind of international power was at work – 'informal empire' – which did not show up on any political map. Argentina, for example, was effectively integrated into the political economy of British capitalism by means which no territorial description could reveal. Indeed, in Gallagher and Robinson's account, not only was this non-territorial empire probably of greater material weight in Britain's international power than was its colonial counterpart, which so dazzled contemporaries by its vast territorial extent; but also, with the exception of a few key sites such as India and South Africa, the conscious preference of successive British governments was more or less consistently for non-territorial over territorial forms of expansion: 'British policy followed the principle of extending control informally if possible and formally if necessary.'[23]

A very similar argument was later made by Gareth Stedman Jones (though hardly by him alone) about the nature of US overseas expansion. 'The *invisibility* of American imperialism', he wrote, was above all attributable to 'its *non-territorial* character' – reinforced secondarily by its consequent ability to find legitimation through 'a *formally anti-imperialist* ideology'.[24]

Yet how far do these phenomena match the supraterritorial quality of globalisation? To find out, let us return to the British case and measure its earliest material sinew – King Cotton – against the territorialist laws of position, distance and separation. How would we identify the territorial location of the early nineteenth-century cotton industry? We could certainly point to the African source of the labour force which was transported to the American South where the raw material was cultivated. We could look at the distribution and sale of the finished product in European countries and – increasingly importantly – in India and beyond. Or of course we could look at the Lancashire factories themselves where the cotton goods were produced by the growing army of wage-labourers drawn from the surrounding English countryside.[25] But if territorialism refers to forms of social organisation which can be positioned on a map, and if, as Scholte insists, 'the mercantile and industrial activity that dominated capitalism during this period operated almost exclusively in territorial space',[26] then the problem should be obvious: where on the map *are* we to position King Cotton? We cannot simply choose one place – say, Lancashire – for then we would not be seeing the social organisation as a whole. Yet nor can we really get round the problem by simply allowing that it occupied a number of separate sites – requiring only that we point to four or five places instead of one. For none of these would have existed without the others.

To come to the point, the reality of the early nineteenth-century cotton industry cannot be described without identifying the way it related all these distant places to each other organically in a single division of labour. Its real (and in fact its only) existence lay in the social and ecological relations by which millions of human lives were interconnected both within these different places and across the vast distances which (territorially) separated them. There is no way of representing those relations as places on a map. If we wanted to give a spatial account of them, then we would have to refer instead to what Donald Lowe called 'the new space of political economy'[27] which emerged towards the end of the eighteenth century – a space defined not by territory but by (inter)relations of production and exchange. And the distance-transcending character of this new space rested not on speed of communication, but rather on the peculiar social properties taken on by human interactions when mediated by the 'exchange-value' of things.

Yet if industrial capitalism generated supraterritoriality in this sense from the start, what about those other two of the latter's defining features, 'transworld simultaneity' and the quality strictly defined as 'transborder'? As to the first of these, we must again shake off the implicit reduction of this phenomenon to a mere function of speed of communication. For, causally speaking, the activity of the Lancashire factories was at every moment premised upon the continuing, simultaneous existence of the American (and other) plantations, and vice versa, irrespective of how long it might have taken for cargo vessels to cross the Atlantic. Indeed, for this reason, Marx – in a metaphor which surely expresses nothing if not wonder at the 'transworld simultaneity' which he was describing – argued that New World slavery had become the 'pedestal' for capitalist development in England, several thousand miles away.[28] And as to the 'transborder' element of global relations, it is clear enough that political borders neither figure in 'the new space of political economy', nor did they place any '*insurmountable* constraints'[29] on the operations of King Cotton. In any case, Scholte himself comes (consistently enough) to the conclusion that this third element does not enjoy quite the same definitional standing as the other two. For he points out that many 'intranational' activities also 'manifest supraterritorial qualities', and therefore merit the designation 'global' even if they cross no borders.

From all this, we may perhaps draw the following preliminary conclusion. Sir Richard Arkwright, cotton-spinner *extraordinaire*, did not, it is true, invent the communications satellite.[30] But then, the communications satellite, it now appears, did not invent supraterritorial space. We have some empirical grounds for supposing that supraterritoriality is not something which has happened to capitalism as the result of late twentieth-century technological advances. It seems rather to be something intrinsic to capitalist social relations themselves. Would it be too much then to suggest that it is rather these social relations which ultimately lie behind the emergence of the communications satellite?

There is, however, a larger, more theoretical point to be drawn out here. On the wilder shores of globalisation theory, these supraterritorial properties and tendencies of capitalism have been taken to point to the ultimate crisis of the nation-state and the states-system. It is an old theme. 'I believe', declared Richard Cobden, speaking for free trade in 1846, 'that if we could be allowed to reappear on this sublunary scene, we should see, at a far distant period, the governing system of this world revert to something like the municipal system.'[31] This is not Scholte's way. For him, globalisation 'shows no sign of erasing the state'. And this is not simply because, having 'unfolded mainly since the 1960s', it needs more time to work its full effects. On the contrary, careful as ever, he has already earlier told us that globalisation, despite being defined as the rise of supraterritorial space, is nonetheless 'not antithetical to territoriality'. However, it *has* 'transcended the territorialist geography that sovereignty presupposes', and as a result it has 'brought the end of sovereignty'.[32] And as we saw earlier, this is not a small thing: three hundred years of the 'Westphalian System' are now over. This is broadly Held's position also, as well as that of other 'transformationalists' in the globalisation debate. We cannot therefore ascribe its apparent equivocations simply to indecisiveness in the mind of an individual author. How then should we explain it? More particularly, can we develop the preceding points about capitalism to explain why this apparent confusion arises as a necessary feature of the folly?

To see how this might be possible, it helps to recall that for Marx the phenomenon of the English cotton industry represented far more than the simple application, however unprecedented, of new technologies to the process of production. Nor could it be understood simply as the rise of an especially effective (or exploitative) mode of surplus appropriation and accumulation, newly released from previously existing social and political restraints. It was both of these things, to be sure. But they in turn were premised upon a deeper, wider and longer-term social transformation which only now, in the new industries, was starting to reveal the scale of its historical potential.

In what was perhaps the most pregnant of his many attempts to formulate clearly the overall nature of this transformation, Marx suggested that the new form of society which it produced could be distinguished from all previous ones in the most fundamental terms: the very 'forms of social connectedness' through which people related to each other, and through which society itself was daily reproduced, had undergone a truly basic shift. The historical norm had been for human societies to be organised and reproduced via 'relations of personal dependence' of one kind or another (benign or otherwise) such as kinship, tribute or even slavery. The Manchester cotton workers, however, whatever the wretchedness of their condition, were tied to each other, to their employers and to their society at large by a quite different form of social connectedness: 'personal independence based on dependence mediated by things'.[33]

The enormous role of American slavery in the rise of King Cotton bears ample witness to the historically, geographically and socially uneven nature of the process of transformation which Marx believed himself to have identified. But he was surely right to hold that in some essential way the future lay more with the generalising of the wage–labour relations emerging in its metropolitan heartlands than with the brutally intensified 'relations of personal dependence' generated at its geographical periphery. At any rate, he devoted by far the greater part of his intellectual effort to drawing out the sociological implications of this new form of human sociation. It was an effort increasingly dominated by a critical engagement with what he took to be the most important – even generative – dimension of this new world: its political economy. But we do well to remember the wider thrust of Marx's argument – that capitalism involves an historical transformation of what Sayer neatly coins 'the elementary forms of social life';[34] for this wider thrust also contains, alongside 'the economics', an argument about the sovereign form of the modern state which reveals how the endless perplexity of the issue of sovereignty for globalisation theory may derive ultimately from the insolubly problematic way in which the category of 'the political' is produced in this modern form of society.

Whatever else it is, capitalism is, like feudalism, a mode of surplus appropriation. And if we want to get to Marx's analysis of sovereignty, we do have to start with this point. For Marx claimed that the ambiguities of sovereignty are rooted in the historically peculiar form that surplus appropriation takes in a capitalist society. And what he thought was peculiar to this form was its organisation via contractual relations of exchange (most importantly of labour-power for wages) among formally legal equals. This was the expression, in the sphere of material relations, of personal independence based on dependence mediated by things. So long as sufficient numbers of people, having no alternative means of subsistence, are compelled by circumstances to sell their labour-power; and so long as those who purchase it are able to employ it profitably, meaning that the product (which they own) embodies a surplus (realised through its sale) over and above the costs which they have invested in its production – so long as these conditions apply, the specifically capitalist form of surplus appropriation is being accomplished. Marx's analysis of capital reaches much deeper than this; and at those deeper levels – where the sociological theory of value is set out – his arguments remain hotly contested and widely rejected. Yet none of those contestations and rejections actually touches the simple descriptive points just made. And those points are already enough to establish the crucial contrast with all societies in which surplus appropriation is organised instead via 'relations of personal dependence'. For in all those other cases, whether the rights of differential appropriation attached to locations in a kinship structure (father, wife, cousin, eldest son) or to positions in a 'politically' defined hierarchy (king, lord, serf) or (as was surely always the case) to some combinations of both of these with yet other forms of social differentiation – in all these cases, those rights and their exercise were always, according to Marx, 'directly social'. That is to say, material claims upon others as individuals were organised and exercised via the explicitly differential social identities with which (for the purposes of social interaction) those individuals were merged.

This may appear at first sight to be an enormous generalisation. Yet for Marx it was an assertion not of some homogeneity of the pre-capitalist world (which was of course almost endlessly various) but rather of the singularity, within any wider historical review, of the modern capitalist form of society. For 'directly social' is the one thing that capitalist relations of production are clearly not. Here, material claims on others are exercised instead via 'private' ownership of the commodities (labour-power and money) which are exchanged and consumed. The dependence remains real enough, but it is mediated by (the exchange of) 'things'. It has radically changed its form. And Marx believed that this was the key to an equally radical change in the very meaning of 'the political'.[35]

For so long as a society is organised via a 'directly social' differentiation of identities (i.e. via 'relations of personal dependence'), the
definitions of kinship, property, and so on, must themselves remain
'directly political'.[36] Consequently, Marx argued, there is in these cases
'as yet no political constitution as distinct from the actual material
state or the other content of the life of the nation'.[37] And it was on the
basis of this that he concluded, in 1843, that '[t]he abstraction of the
political state is a modern product.'[38]

By this he meant that the institutional differentiation of 'the political'
itself, without which the modern idea of the sovereign state was unthink-
able, required nothing less than 'the *dissolution* of the old society', the
abolition indeed of 'the *political character of civil society*'.[39] Or to put it the
other way round, the reorganisation of social life around relations of contractual equality, which uniquely dissolves the traditional dependence of
social orders upon legal and political inequality, has this consequence for
the reconstitution of 'the political' as a dimension of social life:

> It set free the political spirit, which had been, as it were, split up, partitioned
> and dispersed in the various blind alleys of feudal society. It gathered the
> dispersed parts of the political spirit, freed it from its intermixture with civil
> life, and established it as the sphere of the community, the *general* concern of
> the nation, ideally independent of those *particular* elements of civil life.[40]

Marx's language here might seem to endorse a notion of modern politics as actually separate, a self-sufficient sphere comprehensible in its
own terms, independently of the character of the society over which it
presided. That, of course, was the last thing on his mind. For just as the
royal hierarchies and the Estates system of the Middle Ages were the
'political' embodiment and sanction of the 'relations of personal
dependence' characterising that social order, so the same applies
today: the abstract, sovereign form of the modern state which constitutes its citizens as legal and political equals is the political
embodiment and sanction of the new type of social connectedness
characterising capitalism as an historical kind of society: personal independence based on dependence mediated by things.

But if this is what has happened, if the rise of modern sovereignty involved not just the growth of a centralised political apparatus but also, and more crucially, the abstraction of the political itself from its erstwhile role in constituting the 'directly social' relations of pre-capitalist societies, then the real question surely becomes: why should we expect that the transborder extension of any of the (correspondingly *de*-politicised) social relations of the new 'civil society' would undermine the sovereign form of the state? Would we not rather conclude the opposite: namely that here is an historical form of society in which uniquely it becomes possible even for relations of production to extend across political borders precisely *without* affecting the (sovereign) territoriality of the states involved?[41]

If so, then understanding either the domestic or the international relations of the nineteenth century (let alone those of today) would certainly require a different model from that provided by the Westphalian System. To visualise aright our earlier example of the cotton industry, we would perhaps use a concept such as 'social formation' which is not defined in terms of the spaces of national states alone, and which could therefore embrace the actual transnational reach of the interrelations as a geographical whole. But this revisualising would not be purchased at the expense of a geopolitical analysis. For rather than assuming that the importance of transborder connections had dissolved the international moment of the process, we would have to examine how the states whose territories were traversed by these relations were drawn into closer interrelation and conflict by them. And this is exactly the model long ago formulated by Nicos Poulantzas:

> The social formation, which is the nodal point of the expanded reproduction of social relations, tends to intersect the boundaries of the nation-State; and that uneven development which has marked capitalism since its beginnings tends to root itself in, and bring into interrelationship, the nation-States themselves.[42]

Theoretically speaking, has globalisation theory really added anything at all to this formulation? Or has it simply generated a whole new set of confusions due to the Procrustean historical periodisation which its obsession with space has compelled it to adopt? For that is surely how its uncritical endorsement of the idea of the Westphalian System must now strike us.

Be that as it may, we now have enough material to make an initial application of the general hypothesis proposed towards the end of the previous chapter. There we suggested that the embrace of 'globalisation' as a sociological *explanans* must generate insoluble intellectual difficulties. Specifically, it would require a conceptual inflation of 'space' which could neither be grounded in a plausible alternative 'spatial problematic' for social theory, nor be prevented from reifying the very social phenomena which it was attempting to explain. And this, we hypothesised, would either imprison its exposition in intellectual equivocation from the start, or lead to a tacit withdrawal of its central claims by the end.

In Scholte's case, the first of these outcomes is so marked that in a writer less committed to clear expression the intensity of equivocation might even have disguised the source of the problem itself. Yet so determined is he to impose an analytical precision on the concept of globalisation that the basic difficulty with which he wrestles remains visible at each step of the process. The initial need to find a distinctive meaning for the concept drives him to isolate its spatial content, under the heading of 'supraterritoriality'. Once this dimension has been isolated, claims for its transformative impact on the real world become dependent on a conceptual inflation of space into a 'core determinant of social life', for which, however, only a half-hearted argument can plausibly be made. The brief and equivocal attempt to consolidate theoretically this inflated explanatory role for 'space' gives way almost immediately to an uncontrolled relaxation of the definition of 'global'. And from that point on, any independent explanatory significance which the latter term intermittently displays is in fact dependent on an implicit reification of space: the impact of particular kinds of social relationship on the spatial organisation of societies is instead imputed to the social impact of the geographical laws of location, distance and

separation – and their transcendence via increased speed of communication and transport.

The upshot of all this at the level of international theory is an
endorsement of the currently fashionable idea that world politics is
undergoing a transition to a post-sovereign, post-Westphalian system.
Three points may perhaps now be made in conclusion about what a
peculiar destination this actually is.

First, in order to argue that globalisation is a new process with radically transformative implications for the international system, it
clearly helps to have a model of the past in which the inscription of
that process in the very constitution of modern international relations has been rendered invisible. Such a model is indeed provided by
the 'realist' conception of the Westphalian System, the whole force of
which is to produce a definition of the international in terms of
geopolitical norms of interaction between states without reference to
the 'domestic' level of society, where the transnational relations operate.[43] The ironic consequence of this is that globalisation theory,
which prides itself on its intellectual transcendence of 'methodological territorialism', is compelled by the claims it wishes to make about
the present to buy into a quite unsustainably 'territorialist' reading of
the past.

But this is only the beginning. For, secondly, the penalty of this
suppression of the standing of transnational relations in the past must
surely be a misrecognition of their significance in the historical present.

If we work with Marx's historical sociological definition of sovereignty, and the conception of the international system which
Poulantzas drew out of it, then we would expect a proliferation of
transnational relations from the start; we would expect these to grow
very dramatically with the rapid material development and geographical spread of capitalism itself; and we would expect the
temporally and spatially uneven rhythm of this historical process to
generate periodic crises and adjustments in the politics and organisation of the sovereign states system itself, through which this process

is collectively, if anarchically, managed. And this incidentally might help us to understand the events of imperialism, world wars, revolutions and the Cold War which have formed such a prominent feature of modern international history, and yet which do not significantly figure in Scholte's global worldview. What we would not expect, however, is that the simple quantitative increase of these transnational relations, however far it extended, would necessarily signal an incipient transformation of the basic character of the international system itself. For as Poulantzas went on to say, perhaps a little formulaically, '[t]hese frontiers . . . become established as frontiers of the national territory only from the moment when capital and commodities are in a position to break through them.'[44]

If, on the other hand, we really believed that the 'Westphalian model' once (say, before 1900) accurately described an international system which was 'quintessentially territorial', then of course we would find the 'global' statistics of the present day little short of mind-blowing. Nine hundred million telephone lines, two billion radio sets, four hundred and fifty trillion dollars in yearly foreign-exchange turnover, forty-four and a half thousand 'transborder' companies: 'such a large accumulation of data', says Scholte after reeling off a list of sixteen such items, 'surely suggests a significant trend away from territorialist social organization.'[45] To which one can only respond by asking: why, if the data speak so clearly, do the conclusions of Scholte's own work remain so stubbornly equivocal?

Perhaps though, thirdly, we already have the answer to this question. If Scholte believes the Westphalian myth, he cannot fail to be impressed by the statistics. Yet if the Westphalian myth is as misleading as the arguments from Marx and Poulantzas suggest, then those statistics simply will not stack up to produce in the real world the kind of transformation they might seem at first to imply. Scholte's own interpretation of this conundrum appears to waver between a quantitative interpretation – 'much more globalization' is needed to make territorial space finally irrelevant – and a theoretical qualification: 'globalization is not antithetical to territoriality.'[46] But we now have an alternative explanation for why he should find that 'the rise of supraterritoriality shows no sign of producing an end to territoriality.' If it is correct, it would certainly confirm the wisdom of leaving the building of the argument necessarily unfinished. It would provide an answer to the riddle of Scholte's folly.

Does all this mean that a spatio-temporal analysis is of no account for understanding the modern international system? Surely not. David Harvey's *The Condition of Postmodernity* provides one example of such an analysis which not only identifies the historical specificity of the modern capitalist form of space and time, but also, and more specifically, explores the role which bursts of time-space compression have played in the successive geographical reconfigurations of capitalism as a world system which have accompanied its intermittent crises.

Perhaps the most arresting example, however, is that of Poulantzas himself. In *State, Power, Socialism* he devoted a highly suggestive discussion to a comparative analysis of different 'mechanisms of organising social space'. Poulantzas was insistent that 'the historical changes they undergo are not variations on an intrinsic nature, for these mechanisms have no such nature.'[47] Nonetheless, this did not prevent him from attributing considerable explanatory significance to different historical constructions of spatiality. In the case of the capitalist construction, he not only identified the general characteristics we have cited above, but went on to specify political phenomena which, he believed, could not be explained without reference to this new social construction of space. 'Genocide', he argued, 'is . . . a modern invention bound up with the spatialisation peculiar to nation states'[48] – a point he extended into a spatial analysis of 'the roots of totalitarianism'.

But the difference should be clear. Although he chastised his fellow Marxists for assigning only 'a marginal role' to 'transformations of space and time', this did not point to a need for an alternative, spatio-temporal problematic for social theory. The spatial tendencies of different modes of production were indeed a crucial part of their very definition. But *explanans* and *explanandum* remained firmly in their traditional places: 'In whichever way we approach the problem of space, we become aware that space matrices vary with the mode of production and that they are themselves presupposed by the forms of historico-social appropriation and consumption of space.'[49]

3

Rob Walker: Philosophical Backstop?

Introduction

Max Weber famously contrasted the use of words as 'swords against the enemies' with their quite different employment as 'plowshares to loosen the soil of contemplative thought'.[1] And it seems only fair to begin this chapter by acknowledging that in the field of contemporary international theory, there are few, if any, better ploughs than Rob Walker. The imaginative scale of his questions, the simultaneous range and intensity of his textual engagements, the sharpness of his intellectual judgements and the occasional eloquence of the writing itself – all these combine to communicate a sustained intellectual seriousness which has been widely experienced as inspirational. And nowhere are these qualities more in evidence than in his most substantial work – *Inside/Outside: International Relations as Political Theory*. If Walker's only concern was to emphasise that international theory (like any other) rests upon philosophical assumptions which can and should be problematised in various ways, then the success of that work would have to be affirmed unequivocally.

This, however, has not been the only concern. If there is a distinctive motif to his critical enterprise, it is signalled by a heavy repetition of the term 'spatio-temporal' across the surface of his texts. As one would expect of such a writer, this is not just a surface phenomenon.

Albeit hedged about by incessant qualifications and repeated protestations to the reader about the enormous difficulty, and perhaps even impossibility, of the task, the deep foundations have nonetheless been laid of an alternative worldview. And if the themes of space and time have achieved an enduring philosophical cachet in the field of IR theory, this is at least partly due to their ambiguous but highly visible centrality in Walker's work.

Indeed, although he himself has not laid claim to the mantle, it does appear that his publications have come to function as an intellectual backstop for arguments about 'global transformations' couched in more prosaic idioms. It is Walker who is cited by David Held and his fellow authors to support their claim that '[t]he idea of "global politics" challenges the traditional distinctions between domestic/international, inside/outside, territorial/non-territorial politics.'[2] Similarly, Gillian Youngs asserts that among recent literature which has taken up the 'conceptual challenge' of the study of international relations in 'a global age', 'Walker's perspective plays a particular role in highlighting the *deepest aspects* of these crucial, critical developments in the discipline.'[3] In short, claims about the transcendence of the Westphalian System, the emergence of a post-international world, and hence the supersession of the traditional intellectual problematic of the international itself are here being referred for support to the particular historico-philosophical argument about sovereignty and modernity which Walker has made his own.

The reference does not sit entirely easily. For this is an author who explicitly warns against the temptation 'to exaggerate the novelty of novelty',[4] and who declares that both sides in the debate over the erosion of state sovereignty (as well as most reflections on new social movements) are trapped in a discourse of modern politics which is 'possibly the most misleading guide there is' to any future.[5] He makes few assertions of his own about how the world may be changing, resting his argument instead merely on the significance of 'speculations', 'claims' and 'a widespread sense' to this effect. Even the broad affiliation of his work to the camp of 'critical international theory' arrives guarded by a seven-fold qualification, no less.[6] And the intellectual framework of globalisation is itself foresworn in favour of ideas of the 'late- or postmodern'.[7]

Furthermore, in Walker, the easy claims of globalisation theory run up against a writer for whom 'difficulty' is the very index of intellectual seriousness. It is not just that claims about temporal acceleration are 'difficult to interpret', or that 'convincing accounts of alternative possibilities are notoriously difficult to find', or even that 'it is especially difficult . . . to see any clear connection between aspirations for democracy and emerging structures of global power.' These, after all, merely illustrate the general point that 'the contemporary political agenda is full of exceptionally difficult questions.'[8] The real point lies deeper. If the 'guiding theme' of his own writing also 'remains exceptionally difficult to specify except at a very general level', this is because it is itself actually 'motivated . . . by a sense of the difficulty of speaking coherently about politics at this historical juncture' at all. And the reason for that, which really underlies everything else, is that it is 'exceptionally difficult to renounce the security of Cartesian coordinates' which would be required in order to address the question: '. . . if not state sovereignty, . . . what *then*?' 'It is this difficulty,' he warns sternly, at the end of chapter 4, 'not the extravagant presumptions of modernist social science, that demands our attention.'

Globalisation theory, as we have already seen, has its fair share of extravagant presumers. So it is not surprising that this cult of difficulty has opened up a wary textual distance between Walker and his admirers. In the critical international theory literature too, he is more often cited than directly discussed.

Why is it, then, that a prickly customer like Walker, who goes to such lengths to complicate and deflect intellectual incorporation, is nonetheless so happily invoked by globalisation theorists in the field of International Relations? There appear to be three main reasons for this.

First, the substantive claim at the core of Walker's entire work is that the world of territorial sovereignties reflects the privileged role of space in the modern imaginary, a role now challenged by late- or post-modern experiences of temporal accelerations. Because his particular concern is to expose the categorial fixity of international theories as discourses, some scope exists for avoiding any commitment of his own to the concrete claims of globalisation theory. It is usually enough for his purpose to demonstrate that, irrespective of their empirical or theoretical adequacy, they throw into relief 'the enormous authority of spatial imagery'.[9] Still, no amount of prickliness and evasion could hide the fact that the categories of space and time have here (in whatever manner) become central to the explanation of social reality in the way that globalisation theory requires. And in any case, Walker's usual reliance on claims, speculations and intimations itself occasionally gives way to statements of outright empirical affirmation. '[O]urs is an age of speed and temporal accelerations.' We live in 'a world in which boundaries are so evidently shifting and uncertain'. '[B]oth states and capital participate in spatiotemporal processes that are radically at odds with the resolutions expressed by the principle of state sovereignty.' Democratic struggles must respond to 'fundamental rearticulations of spatiotemporal relations'. And even (though the context allows room for manoeuvre on this one): '[T]heories of international relations . . . can be understood as the product of specific historical conditions that have now passed.'[10]

Second, in addition to this general affirmation of spatio-temporal analysis, Walker implicitly advances a special – even strategic – significance for globalisation theory in the field of IR. For international theories are 'a constitutive horizon of modern politics in the territorial state'. As such, they are 'expressions of the limits of the contemporary political imagination' as a whole. '[S]peculations about the accelerative tendencies of contemporary political life' are therefore much more than just speculations: as '[c]hallenges to these limits . . . [they] constitute the crucial condition under which we might be able to renegotiate our understanding of the political under contemporary conditions.'[11]

Even the humblest of globalisation theorists can bask in the reflected glow of that historico-philosophical vocation – so long as they can avoid

framing their speculations in the wrong 'historically specific accounts of
what it means to begin, or to end, or to become other than we are
now'.[12] This last requirement might seem like a heavy caveat indeed,
especially since it 'must lead to the most fundamental questions about
the relation between unity and diversity, self and other and space and
time'.[13] Fortunately, however – and thirdly – this is already 'a crucial
common theme of emerging literatures' which include several of those
out of whose conjunction in the late 1980s the discourse of globalisation theory itself was already emerging. The generously long list of
these emerging literatures includes, among others, those on 'global
political economy, especially in relation to emerging forms of international capital and communications technology . . . the explorations of
at least some kinds of social movements . . . the revalorisation of both
the "local" and the "global"', and so on.[14] And in the footnoted references here and elsewhere, the names of those who would later staff the
academy of globalisation theory – Zygmunt Bauman, David Held, Mike
Featherstone, Scott Lash, and so on – find a ready place.

Later on we shall see that the underlying interdependence between
Walker's work and globalisation theory has an even stronger dimension. For the moment, however, the circumstantial evidence alone is
enough: some embrace globalisation theory of their own free will;
others have it thrust upon them; but the selection of the involuntarily
anointed is not wholly arbitrary. Walker, clearly, does not want to be
anyone's backstop. But when all is said and done, the fact remains that
by invoking a central significance for spatio-temporal analysis, by identifying the international as the strategic site of engagement, and by
referencing many of the scholarly debates in which 'the global' was
already bubbling to the intellectual surface, Walker manoeuvred himself into a position where he was almost bound to end up performing
this role for globalisation theory in International Relations. Can the
backstop hold? In order to find out, we must look more deeply into
Walker's argument.

The investigation which follows has four sections. The first two of
these are expository, as we try to piece together the method and the

substance of Walker's argument in some detail. The third and fourth sections then turn to a critical assessment. And what we shall discover is as follows. Set within a wider intellectual field, the distinctiveness of Walker's position reduces to just two elements: the privileged role which he accords to space in the interpretation of modernity, and his attempt then to derive the problematic of international relations in its entirety from the resultant spatial properties of sovereignty as a political form. By comparing the first of these briefly with the work of Benedict Anderson, we shall try to show how curious this privileging of space actually is – how much it stands in need of a wider intellectual or empirical justification which, however, Walker does not provide. But the bulk of our energies will be directed at that second element, his derivation of the international itself from the modern form of space. For on this, clearly, hangs the issue of whether it is plausible to anticipate the supersession of the condition of 'internationality' itself as a result of the spatio-temporal effects of globalisation. At that point it will be our turn to make an unconventional move. Having implicitly criticised the discipline of IR in the last chapter for its failure to grasp the historical specificity of the modern capitalist international system, we shall seek to place a limit of our own on how far, and in what directions, that critique should be allowed to extend. Indeed, we shall try to use Marx's method of abstraction (as set out in the 1857 'General Introduction') to construct a defence of 'the international' as an intellectual problematic whose object is legitimately and explicitly transhistorical. Walker will certainly give us a good run for our money. But if we succeed in our own constructive exercise, then the support his work can provide for globalisation theory will be severely weakened. And the backstop will fall away.

Ontological Assumptions

Walker's declaration, in the first chapter of *Inside/Outside*, that 'this book has no straightforward thesis or conclusion'[15] does not of course mean that the thesis and conclusion do not exist – only that they will have to be extrapolated by the reader, via a close textual analysis. And for this purpose, Walker does actually supply some clear pointers with which we can begin the operation. 'I insist', he says on page 82, 'that differences between approaches to contemporary world politics must be addressed at the level of basic ontological assumptions.' Again, his own basic ontological assumptions are not explicitly stated. But if we reason from the practice of his texts, we may perhaps draw them out as follows.

First, human beings are self-interpreting creatures, whose behaviour must therefore be understood via the categories through which they construct the meaningfulness of their existence. Second, all such constructions must grapple with 'three philosophical problems' which attend human existence as such.[16] These problems are summarised as the problem of universality and particularity, the problem of self and other, and the problem of space and time. Third, human beings are social animals in the deep sense that the 'resolution' of these problems is achieved inter-subjectively in the form of (historically various) cultures.

It is presumably from these three ontological assumptions that Walker (again implicitly) derives what in effect will operate as the key methodological premise of his argument: all human societies embody (and may fruitfully be studied as) historically and culturally specific 'resolutions' of the aforementioned existential problems. This seems reasonable enough. Yet why, it might be asked, should we endorse these particular ontological assumptions rather than others? Although Walker is very cagey about formalising any explanatory dimension to his 'meditations', the persistence with which he returns to these philosophical problems cannot avoid an attribution of significance: he must, in short, believe that the specific discursive forms in which different cultures embody resolutions to these problems are in some crucial way foundational for their wider character as social formations. We should therefore clarify exactly what these problems are.

What Walker describes as the problem of the particular and the universal is effectively the same as Plato's problem of the Many and the One.[17] Its significance lies not simply in the local cognitive challenge which it generates – how the variety of concrete particulars can be subsumed by the mind under general categories – but more profoundly in the existential need which it reflects of humans as reasoning subjects: making sense of our experience is the condition – even the substance – of its construction as meaningful. And this is why, for Plato as well as for Walker, the problem of the universal and the particular is simultaneously a technical challenge to the construction of explanation and a mystical challenge to the construction of identity.

For Walker, however, as a political theorist analysing 'approaches to contemporary world politics', the general problem of the universal and particular recurrently finds expression also in a more precise inflection: the same constructions of culture which may provide a meaningful resolution of the problem *within* a given community serve to reproduce and reinforce the problem on a different plane. For modern 'world politics' subsumes a known empirical diversity of cultural solutions. And on this plane, the problem is therefore reopened as an insoluble tension between the claims of cultural particulars (now known to be particulars) and those of the human (now known to extend beyond any culturally specific resolution).

On the basis of this, we can readily see the purchase of the second 'philosophical problem' – that of self and other, or inside and outside. If the ontological problem of the universal and the particular is resolved within a given cultural community, then a different ontological status necessarily attaches to what lies outside that community, a difference which will be reflected at the level of collective identity in a mutually defining opposition of self and other. Walker would rightly assert that the problem of self and other, or inside and outside, is 'not specific to international relations alone'.[18] Nonetheless, there is no denying that in this domain it will have a special prominence. Moreover, it seems reasonable to assume that the actual content of the dichotomies of self/other and inside/outside will vary historically with the particular cultural forms in which the earlier problem of the universal and the particular is 'resolved'. And indeed, central to Walker's analysis of 'modernity' as a culture is a claim that this particular resolution renders the problem of self and other especially intractable.

Finally, there is the problem of space and time. 'Reified temporal horizons', says Walker, 'give meaning to where we think we may be going.'[19] And this is also existentially necessary to human beings if the twin threats of ceaseless change and individual mortality are to be subsumed into an account of life as meaningful. Meanwhile, 'ideas of space, like those of time, express many of the greatest mysteries of human existence.'[20] The statement is a little coy; but if we combine it with a later claim that 'the spatial constructs associated with Euclid and Newton played a decisive role in determining the cultural forms of European civilisation,'[21] then the scale of the overall point is clear enough: cultural communities do not simply exist in space and time; they are in some part produced through specific constructions of space and time as meaningful.

If these are the 'basic ontological assumptions' of Walker's analysis, the next step must be their application in the analysis of concrete historical worlds. 'I affirm', he says, 'the priority of history.'[22] And sure enough, an implied narrative now emerges, opening up into a triptych of medieval, early modern/modern and late-modern/postmodern mental and material universes.

Walker does not give us much to go on with regard to the first of these.[23] But we may perhaps reconstruct its outlines as follows. In the (European) Middle Ages, the coordinating intellectual 'resolution' was the specific achievement of 'scholastic universalism'.[24] In this idiom, 'hierarchical modes of knowing and being'[25] were articulated around the central motif of the Great Chain of Being. This motif 'permitted accounts of a world of continuities, a culture of resemblances, an ethics of greater and lesser, and thus of a politics rooted ultimately in a monotheistic theology'.[26] The spatial correlate of this was reflected in 'the complex overlapping jurisdictions of the medieval era',[27] while the 'reified temporal horizon' was not defined by the forward movement of linear time as History; rather,

> time, and movement . . . came to a stop at the edges of eternity, somewhere among the angels crowded on the almost but never quite infinite point of transition from here to there, from life to death, from the City of Man to the City of God.[28]

The lack of any detailed specification beyond these broad intimations (accompanied by the odd, wandering allusion to 'feudal modes of production') presumably reflects the fact that Walker's interest lies overwhelmingly with the crystallising of the modern era which followed. And since it is his treatment of this which in fact determines his later uneasy but unavoidable rendezvous with globalisation theory, we must look the more carefully into it.

Space and Modernity

The gist of Walker's argument may be approached by triangulating three characteristic claims. The first of these is that the principle of state sovereignty constitutes 'the crucial modern political articulation of all spatiotemporal relations'.[29] The second is that this monolithic status of sovereignty derives from a specific role which it plays in the culture of modernity. For 'sovereignty can be read as a very elegant and specifically modern resolution of [the] three philosophical problems' which we earlier saw to be rooted in the character of human existence as such – problems of the universal and the particular, of inside and outside, and of space and time.[30] And finally, what makes sovereignty 'specifically modern' is the fact that it expresses 'the spatial resolution of all philosophical options'.[31] With claims such as these in the air, it is hardly surprising that the globalisation theorists should scent a whiff of philosophical profundity in their endeavours. And

Walker, it must be said, gives them every encouragement: 'if it is true', he adds, 'that contemporary political life is increasingly characterised by processes of temporal acceleration, then we should expect to experience increasingly disconcerting incongruities' between the emerging realities and traditional theories of world politics.[32] But what exactly does Walker mean by his claims about the role and character of sovereignty?

The answer is at once historical and philosophical. For Walker directs our attention to early modern Europe, where he locates the crystallising of the idea of sovereignty within the ferment of a wider cultural crisis. The essence of this crisis (itself the product of 'processes that had already been underway for a considerable period')[33] was that the medieval 'world of hierarchies and continuities' was giving way to the modern 'world of autonomies and separations'.[34] This was reflected not only in the breakdown of the political structure of Christendom, but also in the simultaneous dissolution of its spiritual and intellectual frameworks in the face of the scientific revolution. In such a context, the existential resolution previously secured by the Great Chain of Being ceased to function. '[A]ttempts to construct an account of political life'[35] required a new resolution. And somewhere along the line from Machiavelli (whose assertion of secular autonomy was still 'predicated on an archaic cosmology'[36]) and Hobbes (in whom it is instead predicated on 'the Euclidean–Galilean principle of absolute space'[37]) the new resolution emerged. The concept and practice of sovereignty are the expression in the sphere of politics of the 'decisive role' played by the idea of absolute space in determining the wider 'cultural forms of European civilisation'.[38] From this point on, 'modern politics is a spatial politics',[39] participating in, even constituting the lynchpin of, a wider resolution of existential questions and answers in spatial terms.

How then does it work? How can absolute political space, which severs, excludes, empties and homogenises, serve as an integrative principle of cultural meaning? This, for Walker, is the 'elegance', the 'style' and indeed the 'metaphysical achievement' of sovereignty.[40]

First in line is the problem of the universal and the particular. This receives a double resolution. On the one hand, the existence of a (worldwide) sovereign states-*system* allows for the persistence and embrace of cultural particularity within a universal framework of norms of interaction (however minimal). On the other hand, the (cross-cultural) generalising of the sovereign state as a particular cultural form could be reinterpreted as the realisation of a universal human necessity – for security, or freedom, or development. '[O]ne system, many states'[41] becomes the spatially defined formula by which the problem of the Many and the One is resolved in modern world politics.

This 'primary resolution' both enables and depends upon an absolute spatial demarcation of inside and outside, self and other. Within the legitimised particularity of individual states, 'it becomes possible to aspire to the universal' – to realise, on the basis of a stable, overarching authority, common human aims of 'reason and justice, democracy and liberty' which could not be envisaged in its absence.[42] The very terms of this possibility, however, dictate the corresponding impossibility of its extension beyond the borders of the sovereign state. There, the sway of contingency and the clash of particulars reign supreme. The spatially absolute demarcation of inside and outside is thus from the start invested with a philosophically absolute demarcation of human possibility and obligation – a demarcation reflected simultaneously in the canonical demarcation (and irreconcilable ontological assumptions) of the literatures of political theory and international theory.

Finally, this same demarcation is the key to understanding how sovereignty 'resolves', by reconfiguring, the problem of space and time. For the spatially demarcated spheres of inside and outside are also the sites of contrasted temporalities. Inside, the cumulative realisation of social aspirations allows time – past, present and future – to be 'tamed', that is, interpreted as the unfolding medium of human meaning: Progress. Outside, it is condemned to a drama of 'recurrence and repetition'[43] in which only the identification of tragic circularities can stave off the yet worse experience of time as ultimately directionless and therefore incapable of expressing any meaning at all for humankind at this, its most inclusive level of existence. In this way, the practice of sovereignty is 'a discourse of eternity', in which the imaginative limit previously expressed in the theological line between the temporal and the eternal now reappears along the spatial demarcation of inside/outside. And international theory, wittingly or not, becomes the carrier of heavy existential questions which it can answer only with 'a paean to a temporality without hope of redemption'.[44]

Two further steps complete the overall structure of Walker's argument. Although they are broken up and scattered across the work as a whole, logical clarification requires – and the substance of his claims allows – their reassembly and insertion at this point. In the first step, Walker derives what are conventionally assumed to be the properties of 'the international' in general from the historically specific 'resolutions' of early modern Europe. In the second, he anticipates the undermining of these resolutions – and hence of 'the international' – by 'fundamental rearticulations of spatiotemporal relations'.[45] We shall summarise each of these in turn.

It is Walker's contention that the existence of a discrete sphere of 'international ethics' is not rooted in any general problematic framed by the interaction of a plurality of political communities. Rather it 'arises directly from this spatiotemporal resolution' which we have just reviewed.[46] And although one can find points at which this claim appears to be qualified, or even contradicted,[47] there is no doubting the intended overall thrust of the argument. 'The principle of sovereignty alone', he reiterates on page 67, 'is sufficient to generate the characteristic problematic of ethics and international relations.' And this is followed up by a climactic, head-on dismissal of any notion of a general 'problematic of the international'. Against those who would claim that something of sovereignty is rooted in the wider issues of the pre-existing fragmentation of humanity into a multiplicity of interacting communities, Walker responds with an extremely bold inversion. Sovereignty, he says, is not simply a formalisation of international fragmentation. It is, first and foremost, a spatial resolution of the relation between universality and particularity. International fragmentation is only one consequence of this resolution, the other being an account of political community and temporal progress within the state.[48]

Now, if geopolitical fragmentation is – so far from being a cause – only a consequence through which the effects of a spatial resolution of existence are refracted at the level of politics, then it should be possible to reinterpret the central themes of IR theory and practice as – ultimately – emanations of this spatial resolution. And this is what Walker next seeks to do, identifying four consequences of 'viewing the state in essentially spatial terms', and five problem areas in IR theory which reflect the permanent and increasing difficulty of screwing the lid of spatial definition tightly onto the reality of world politics.[49]

The four consequences comprise in effect an intellectual straitjacket by which attempts to conceptualise the possibility of historical change in the sphere of international relations are constricted. Briefly, 'threats to the territorial integrity of the state' recurrently provoke over-hasty claims as to its demise as an historical form; proposed alternatives to the state fail to disentangle themselves from its underlying spatio-temporal mainspring and therefore simply generalise the latter into some form of (sovereign) world government; and finally, so rigidly does the spatial definition of politics suppress the imagination of temporal movement that debates sparked by 'novelty in the structure of the international system' are condemned to a useless oscillation: 'Either Thucydides and Hobbes merely require a few footnotes to bring them up to date, or the globalist millennium is just around the corner.'[50]

Meanwhile, change or no change, the absolute spatial definition of sovereign politics already generates the sphere of the international as intrinsically problematic: it is the very composition of the international by sovereign states which renders its anarchical, violent character by definition irremediable. Consequently, for IR, 'sovereignty is both constitutive of the system and a problem to be overcome.'[51] And it is this which then explains the clustering of (once again, necessarily inconclusive) disciplinary debates around such issues as international law, intervention, international organisation, and so on. These issues are, Walker freely acknowledges, already 'quite familiar to students of international relations'.[52] That is, indeed, his whole point: so long as the sovereign resolution of spatio-temporal relations subsists, they can be neither avoided nor overcome. And what he adds to these debates is the realisation (once again) that their conundrums are rooted not in a general problematic of the international but rather in an historically specific, spatially defined resolution of the mysteries of human existence.

Into this already troubled landscape, the 'temporal accelerations' now start to intrude. They move, it seems, to the rhythm of a different historical universe, one which does not yet even fully exist, but whose very intimations introduce a new and increasingly discordant strain of determinations into the experience of the present.

Exactly what are they? If we concentrate on the empirical (rather than textual) phenomena that Walker invokes, we find that they are effectively twofold. First, there is the momentous year 1989, which triggered 'the simultaneous dissolution of Cold War geopolitics and rapid entrenchment of a globally organised capitalism across the territorial divisions of Europe'.[53] For all its sound and fury, however, 1989 was in fact a product of 'accelerative tendencies' which form 'the most distinctive characteristic of the [twentieth] century' as a whole.[54] If we ask in turn what form these tendencies take, the answer seems to be a combination of 'global flows of capital' and 'contracting response times' for defence planners due to the forward march of military technology.[55] The cumulative effect of these is a deepening

> contradiction – or perhaps it is just an incongruity – between structures of power that seem to be increasingly internationalised, globalised, in some sense universalised and processes of participation, representation, accountability and legitimation that remain rooted in the institutionalised apparatuses of states.[56]

When we add in Walker's recognition that 'powerful claims about change, novelty and transformation' have in fact been central to European social and political thought 'for at least two hundred years',[57] then the historical narrative on which Walker's 'accelerative tendencies' rest becomes fully apparent. It starts at the time of the Enlightenment and the industrial revolution; it is driven forwards by the social and technological dynamics of capitalism; and its direction is towards more and more intense forms of global interdependence, which increasingly problematise notions of politics drawn from the antecedent, early modern period.

One might have thought that Walker, like Scholte and Held in the last chapter, has arrived rather late in the historical day to be issuing predictions about the coming obsolescence of seventeenth-century political theory. What this actually tells us, however, is just how deeply laid he believes the ontological assumptions of early modern thought to be within the political culture of modernity. And this in turn explains why the embrace by Walker of globalisation theory and vice versa (though sealed, as we shall soon confirm, by a mutual intellectual dependence) must indeed be an 'exceptionally difficult' one. If it is indeed the *longue durée* of the 'three resolutions' which is now finally ending, then claims about the demise of sovereignty which do not engage with 'the most fundamental questions about the relation between unity and diversity, self and other and space and time'[58] will simply reconfirm the useless oscillation mentioned above. No-one, not even Walker, has answers to these questions. The best he can propose is an empirical survey of new social movements to see if any of them manifests new spatio-temporal forms of existence.[59] He ploughs the field. He cannot sow the seed. And it is not at all clear whether many of the globalisation theorists are not themselves of the sod that needs to be turned.

To summarise then: all human societies embody and reproduce historically specific resolutions to problems that attend human existence as such; modernity is defined as one such social and philosophical resolution of these – above all, a uniquely spatial resolution; the key political expression of this is the institutional form of sovereignty which simultaneously generates both the inside and the outside of modern politics. It is the key to explaining not just the *form* of the international, but its very existence. The contemporary transformations invoked by globalisation theory are indeed threatening to unhinge the foundations of modern culture. But to understand what these transformations really are, how far they have proceeded and what future they may be bringing – all this is impossible so long as we remain trapped within the discursive universe of sovereignty which, precisely because it reaches so deep, has not only occupied the heartland of our political practice but also colonised our ability to imagine alternative futures which do not partake of the existing spatio-temporal resolution.

Why Space?

Well, what are we to make of all this? Perhaps the first point to note is that while Walker's position certainly has its idiosyncrasies, its obscurity or originality is by no means as great as its critics or admirers have tended to imply. Its overall provenance is that of philosophical anthropology – the comparative study of what Max Weber called 'the inner meaning' of different cultural ways of being human. Its premise is soteriological – asserting the significance for social life as a whole of how (via categories of redemption, salvation and transcendence) particular cultures resolve existential contradictions into a mystical basis of meaningful experience. And its purchase on the common enterprise of the social sciences lies in its interrogation of 'modern', 'Western' culture in these terms, revealing the special difficulty of the latter's attempts to provide secular resolutions of existential problems everywhere else redeemed in a theological idiom.

That this approach can indeed be used to generate profound insights into the modern condition is not to be doubted, as we may confirm by recalling one of its most celebrated recent applications: Benedict Anderson's *Imagined Communities*.[60] Published a full decade before *Inside/Outside*, Anderson's work moved magisterially across a very similar terrain to that later covered by Walker. It, too, turned for its explanatory starting point to the 'fatalities of existence' and the ways in which different cultures offered 'redemption from them'.[61] It elaborated this premise into a method of discursive analysis which understood the institutional forms of human societies (as well as their cultural ideas) to embody particular resolutions of these fatalities. Anderson, too, took the bearings of modern political community by sourcing its emergence within the historical dissolution of the theological resolution provided by Christendom:

> Disintegration of paradise: nothing makes fatality more arbitrary. Absurdity of salvation: nothing makes another style of continuity more necessary. What then was required was a secular transformation of fatality into continuity, contingency into meaning.[62]

And, last but not least, Anderson was fully and eloquently alive to the ways in which the specifically sovereign imagining of political community partook of and expressed historically new constructions of the meaningfulness of space and time.

In all this, it should be added, Anderson effectively reproduced and extended the method deployed by Max Weber, both in the latter's general soteriology of the World Religions, and in its substantive application to 'the specific and peculiar Western form of rationalism'.[63] Indeed, in so doing, he carried it in one vital respect beyond what Weber himself had been able to achieve. For nationalism, as has been pointed out elsewhere, had remained perhaps *the* greatest lacuna in Weber's sociological writings. Comparing Weber with Ernest Gellner on this count, Perry Anderson observed: 'Whereas Weber was so bewitched by the spell of nationalism that he was never able to theorize it, Gellner has theorized nationalism without detecting the spell.'[64] The achievement of *Imagined Communities* in this respect was that it succeeded in deploying the soteriological method in such a way that the spell itself finally became the object of compelling theoretical analysis.

All this being so, we now have to answer the following question: if the spatio-temporal specificity of sovereignty has already been identified, and if its analysis has already been incorporated within a wider soteriological account of the historical transition from medieval to modern forms of consciousness and social practice, wherein lies the distinctiveness of Walker's position? The answer to this is twofold: first, his particular emphasis on space; and second, his interpolation of the question of the international.

As to the first of these, it must be said that in the light of Anderson's work (and *a fortiori* that of Weber), Walker's emphasis on space starts to look strange indeed. Modern politics, he has told us, 'is a spatial politics'. Well, it may be true that the rise of modern cultural forms involves a reconceptualising of space as absolute and abstract, or 'inviolable and sharply delimited'.[65] The trouble is, exactly the same could be said of time, whose distinctively modern conceptualisation as irreversible, linear and uniform invests it with the same quality of being 'inviolable and sharply delimited'. 'So deep-lying is this new idea', says Benedict Anderson, 'that one could argue that every essential modern conception is based on a conception of "meanwhile".'[66] Yet this does not lead Anderson to insist that modern politics is a *temporal* politics. (Conversely, and even earlier, Poulantzas had explicitly used the inside/outside couplet to analyse the territoriality of the modern state without, however, allowing it to achieve the conceptually overweening role which it assumes in Walker's work.[67])

And understandably so, for it is not only space and time which partake of these properties of uniformity and abstraction. On the contrary, for classical social theory, it was precisely the generalising of these properties across the totality of forms of social reproduction (mental and material) which defined the key question – the question of modernity itself. Abstraction of individuals *as* 'individuals', of space and time as 'emptiable', of states as 'sovereign', of things as 'exchange-values' – we moderns, wrote Marx, 'are now ruled by *abstractions*'.[68]

In the face of this proliferation of abstractions, one might want to pause a little before rushing in and naming any single one as determinant. The 'absolute' territorial definition of modern politics might, after all, itself be just one expression of a cultural 'resolution' by no means confined to, or (therefore) definable in terms of, 'the spatial'. Perhaps Max Weber and Benedict Anderson paused too long. For them, rationalisation and disenchantment remained a composite historical process; ultimately there was no fixed causal hierarchy among the parts, however much they all increasingly manifested and accelerated the unified cultural distillate of secularisation. But at least this enabled them to take a wider, empirically open, cross-cultural measure of the process as a whole. Walker's position, by contrast, appears to confound a debatable substantive claim that spatiality became the uniquely dominant idiom of early modern European culture with a conclusion which would not necessarily follow even if the substantive claim were correct – namely that spatial categories thenceforth assume a corresponding causal priority in historical and sociological explanation and analysis.

Even if one agrees, as Donald Lowe does, that 'immanent, rational spatial representation was the dominant epistemic order' in early modern Europe,[69] the notion that this continued (like the supposed Westphalian System) undisturbed by the emergence of capitalist society would be extraordinary. At the very least, one would need some account of how that earlier 'episteme' became heavily overdetermined by 'the new space of political economy'. Such a recognition, however, would unhinge Walker's argument just as surely as it earlier exposed the liabilities of Scholte's (and Held's) acceptance of the Westphalian narrative. For it would then once again become apparent that modern capitalist sovereignty cannot be so straightforwardly derived from its (pre-capitalist) early modern antecedent. And the temporal accelerations of 'late- or post-modernity' would correspondingly acquire a real history within the very 'spatio-temporal resolution' which they are supposedly working to dissolve. Placed in this light, the shadow cast by Walker's argument starts indeed to pick out the craggy lines of the folly analysed in the last chapter.

It was of course fashionable in the early 1990s to make such arguments, in the cross-over debates of post-structuralism and early globalisation theory. Anderson himself registered the mood in the new chapters added to the second edition of *Imagined Communities*.[70] Now that the fashion has passed, however, it is difficult to see what durable intellectual justification it has left behind. *Why space?* Every variation of globalisation theory presupposes that there can be a sociologically or philosophically plausible answer to this question. If it exists, however, it is not to be found in the work of Rob Walker. Invocations of mystery are all very well, but as Nietzsche once pointed out, they will hardly suffice on their own. 'Mystical explanations are considered deep,' he wrote in *The Gay Science*. 'The truth is, they are not even superficial.'[71] And the placement of this aphorism, directly after the parable of the madman who announced the death of God, gives it a singular relevance here.

But if we cannot yet explain the rationale for this prioritising of space, we can certainly diagnose its intellectual effects. And nowhere are these more visible, or more problematic, than in the second area of Walker's distinctiveness, his account of the international.

The Problematic of the International

Here, once again, we are faced first with the problem of clarifying exactly where the distinctiveness of Walker's contribution lies. Taken at face value, his own claims that 'the principle of state sovereignty has received relatively little analytical attention',[72] or that the mutually reinforcing separation between the canons of domestic and international political theory has, likewise, 'attracted remarkably little attention'[73] – such claims, if they are not to be treated simply as moments of unguarded hubris, must appear quite extraordinary.

For the problems generated for relations among political communities by the absolute, exclusive form of the sovereign state, and the impossibility therefore of constructing an international theory by simply extending the precepts of (domestic) political theory 'proper', have, if anything, been *the* defining claims of International Relations as an academic problematic. These claims have had their historical treatments – which have generally placed the genesis of the modern system of states in the same historical conjuncture as does Walker. And they have had their canonical meditations too. The most famous of these, by Martin Wight in 1966, clearly identified the contrasted temporalities of (linear) progress inside and (cyclical) 'recurrence and repetition' outside the state, noting that they were each held in place by 'the prejudice of the nation-state' – a category of whose historical and cultural specificity he was manifestly, if idiosyncratically, aware.

Twelve years later a remarkable counterblast was sounded from within the same intellectual tradition. Michael Donelan turned Martin Wight on his head. Where Wight had ended by judging the mutual exclusions of domestic and international theory to be logically irreversible, Donelan started out, in effect, by declaring these same exclusions to be the abiding moral and intellectual scandals of each field. Using the apparently whimsical literary form of an imagined pub conversation among the great political theorists from Aristotle to Marx, Donelan in fact arraigned the entire classical canon of Western political philosophy in the sternest possible terms: if international theory was incapable of getting beyond a worldview peopled by states rather than by human beings, the ultimate cause of this lay with the political theorists themselves; for at the deepest level they had presupposed, as the unacknowledged condition of their accounts of 'the good life', that human life is pursued only within particularist political communities. So far had they naturalised this assumption that they had successfully evaded responsibility for its primary consequence: they felt no obligation to write about the international sphere which their own underlying assumption had generated as a moral 'wasteland between states'.[74] Donelan, however, has had enough of this. He forces them to speak, to say how they would justify their assumption. In the back and forth which follows, the problem of inside and outside is tied back into the great philosophical themes which Walker, too, had foregrounded: the Many (political communities) and the One (humanity), fatality and transcendence (or as Donelan puts it, 'Nature and Grace'[75]), the 'tremendous dichotomy of European thought' associated with Descartes,[76] and so on. And by the close of the evening, Donelan is plainly not satisfied with what he has heard. For he ends by proposing the outright abandonment of the unargued assumption on which he claims the entire tradition of Western political philosophy is resting.

Thus, as Lene Hansen concluded, '[a]n analysis of state sovereignty is not a novel idea introduced by Walker. Portraying the domestic and international as two distinct realms was not invented by Walker either.'[77] Nor, we may now add, was the recognition of the mutual constitution of these two realms and of their attendant discourses.

Thus, in his periodising of the emergence of the modern states-system, his emphasis on the unbridgeable chasm thenceforth dividing domestic and international, and his identification of the kinds of ethical and practical dilemmas which international theory faces, Walker seems almost at one with the most conventional of 'realist' approaches to the subject. And yet, for all that, when Roy Jones pointed this out in a highly critical review of *Inside/Outside*, Walker was right to draw attention to the 'degree of parody' involved in his own critique of the field.[78] For he had never actually claimed that orthodox international theory did not accurately and even poignantly reflect the experience of modern international politics. On the contrary, he saw it as a crucial part of the discursive construction and reproduction of that experience. His own diagnosis was therefore fated to move within the same orbit, to pick out the same shapes and work with the same received materials as it went about its business of uncovering the key rhetorical moves, intellectual elisions and ontological exclusions which made up the inner workings of the discourse.

It comes down, then, to this: if Walker can lay a claim to distinctiveness, it lies not in his identification of the problems encountered under the sign of the international, but rather in his account of where they come from. For Donelan, these problems arise out of the enduring division of humanity into a plurality of political communities, and they are exacerbated by the failure of Western political theory to engage seriously with this division. He propounds, that is, the elements of a transhistorical problematic of the international. And this is what Walker is perhaps most at pains to reject. For him, these same problems, while real enough, are only occluded by being referred to any transhistorical problematic of division, fragmentation or anarchy. As he tries to illustrate at one point with reference to the classical Greek *polis*, the political meaning of inside and outside has no fixed determinacy; it varies according to the prior cultural resolutions of existential problems which differently colour the life of different historical societies. For him, therefore, the problems of the international cannot be derived from any transhistorical template: the very existence of the international and its problems is instead rooted in the historically specific resolutions of early modern Europe.

Thus, while Donelan presents 'the Historicists' as late entrants to his imagined conversation, who succeed only in providing a further iteration of the general problem in a new form, Walker, affirming 'the priority of history', invokes Marx and accuses IR theory of producing 'Robinsonades'.

Which of them is right? A great deal hangs on this question. If Walker is correct, then the anticipation by globalisation theory of a post-international world in which traditional IR theory is rendered anachronistic has real plausibility. If, on the other hand, the problematic of the international is not entirely reducible to its modern form, then the danger is clear enough: grounded in an illicit conflation of the general with the particular, arguments for a post-international world would merely deprive their exponents of a necessary dimension for explaining contemporary world politics.

It is this latter possibility which we are now going to explore. In doing so, we shall be seeking an answer to the question raised in the

Introduction to this book: in the face of the new theoretical framework presupposed by globalisation theory, we may well wish to defend the claims of classical social theory, but do we want to defend International Relations in some way as well? What, if anything, is worth preserving in the traditional idea of a distinctive problematic of the international? Since we spent much of the last chapter criticising the reification of that problematic in the distorted historical claims of the Westphalian syndrome, even contemplating a positive answer to this question might seem a peculiar, even perilous, next step to take. Yet take it we must. For, to put the matter in a schematic form which will hopefully become clearer in the course of what follows: the answer to a false generalising of the (historically) particular into (transhistorical) universals cannot be found in an equally false collapsing of a (transhistorical) universal into an (historically specific) particular. In this intellectual error, we shall argue, lie both the ultimate source of Walker's 'difficulty', and an enormous trap which, all unawares, globalisation theory has laid for itself.

To begin, then: Walker's use of Marx's term 'Robinsonades' – drawn from the 1857 'General Introduction' – is entirely apposite. For the criticism he wants to make of IR theory at this point is almost identical in its form to that made by Marx of classical political economy. Just as the IR theorists seek to explain modern international relations as a simple expression of a general (i.e. transhistorical) anarchical condition of geopolitics, so the political economists had attempted to explain modern capitalist production as an expression of 'the *general* [i.e. transhistorical] *preconditions* of all production'.[79] And the results had been the same. On the one hand, wrote Marx, precisely because those 'general preconditions' were derived by abstracting from every real historical form of production (in order to produce categories which apply universally), the resultant problematic of 'production in general . . . reduces itself in fact to a few very simple characteristics, which are hammered out into flat tautologies'.[80] And with these, of course, 'no real historical stage of production can be grasped'.[81] On the other hand, this intellectual

impoverishment of the categories of political economy had consequences (even, Marx thought, purposes) which were far more than
intellectual in nature. For it ended by presenting production – all
production – as 'encased in eternal natural laws independent of history, at which opportunity *bourgeois* relations are then quietly
smuggled in as the inviolable natural laws on which society in the
abstract is founded.'[82]

This last point, in fact, does not need to be framed conspiratorially.
Since the 'general preconditions' are derived by individuals concretely
located in a given historical world, no conscious purpose is required to
explain how the abstractions they produce carry the marks of that
world. For that is necessarily where they start from; it is 'what is given,
in the head as well as in reality, and . . . these categories therefore
express the forms of being'[83] of that same world. Robinson Crusoe
may have been 'abstracted' by shipwreck from the physical environment of bourgeois society; the consequence, however, of this novelistic
thought-experiment was not the uncovering of a universal, pre-social
human nature, but rather the representation as natural, pre-social
and universal of the particular social determinations 'given in the
head' of the author (or, to allow some justice to Defoe, in the heads of
the vast majority of his readers).

Just as for Marx, the effect of such Robinsonades as those of political economy was to obliterate the historical specificity of capitalism –
and with it, the key to explaining the novel experiences of modernity – so something very similar applies with Walker: the effect of
deriving the experience of modern international politics from a general, transhistorical problematic of anarchy is to obliterate the
historical specificity of sovereignty as a spatio-temporal resolution –
and with it, the key to explaining the discursive construction of
modern politics around the absolute spatial polarities of inside and
outside. And matters are only made worse by the fact that, just as for
Marx, the general abstraction of 'the international' is no more than
an unwitting extrapolation from the modern case, which therefore
inscribes as eternal, natural laws of geopolitics what is in fact peculiar

to the latter. Truly, the intellectual core of both these discourses is all smoke and mirrors.

Unlike Walker, however, Marx did not simply leave it at that. If he dismissed 'the unimaginative conceits of the eighteenth-century Robinsonades',[84] he steered equally clear of what initially looks like their obvious methodological antidote. It did not follow, he cautioned, 'that in order to talk about production at all we must either pursue the process of historic development through its different phases, or declare beforehand that we are dealing with a specific historic epoch.'[85] The problem with general abstractions, it turns out, lies not in their inherent inadmissibility, but rather in the particular manner in which they are brought into relation with more narrowly historical categories. In fact, Marx argues, it is *only* by combining historically specific categories *with* general abstractions that the explanatory power of the former is realised.

Thus, in the course of the same argument which weighs so heavily against the Robinsonades, we find Marx himself simultaneously insisting that 'all epochs of production have certain common traits', that some 'determinations belong to all epochs', and indeed even that '[n]o production will be thinkable without them.'[86] How then can these apparently divergent injunctions (to attend simultaneously to the universal and the particular) be aligned within a unitary explanatory method? Marx's implicit answer to this question illustrates the general character of the issues involved by momentarily switching focus from the study of production to the study of language:

> [E]ven though the most developed languages have laws and characteristics in common with the least developed, nevertheless, just those things which determine their development, i.e. the elements which are not general and common, must be separated out from the determinations valid for all production [*sic*] as such, so that in their unity . . . their essential difference is not forgotten.[87]

Unity *and* difference: the transhistorical and the historically specific can – and indeed must – be combined in the analysis of any concrete particular. Without this self-conscious combination (which presupposes their prior analytical differentiation) the specific determinations of any actual historical form of production cannot be fixed: either they are falsely dissolved into the properties of production in general, or they are inflated beyond recognition by absorbing into themselves determinations which are in fact 'common to all stages of production'. Thus we can already see that it is possible, in principle, to push an argument about historical specificity too far.

Marx is still not quite done, however, with the general and the particular. To what we might call the diachronic conjunction of these two in the analysis of any concrete historical form, he now appends its synchronic equivalent. For in order to constitute 'production' as an object of analysis, it is necessary not only to fix its particular historical forms in relation to its general transhistorical characteristics; we must also (whether as a general category or in any of its varying historical forms) distinguish production as a particular dimension in relation to the wider processes of social reproduction in general. Of what nature, then – for this is the question Marx moves directly on to in the second section of this text – is 'the general relation of production to distribution, exchange [and] consumption'?[88] And his answer here parallels in a synchronic register the earlier formula for relating the transhistorical and the historical:

> The conclusion we reach is not that production, distribution and exchange are identical, but that they all form the members of a totality, distinctions within a unity.[89]

There it is again – the painstaking effort to avoid collapsing the general and the particular into each other (in either direction), the insistence nonetheless that it is only in their analytical conjunction that the determinations identified by either can be brought into a clear focus.

To conclude this excursus, it is presumably on the basis of all this, by aligning the twin crosshairs of this method, that Marx, the lambaster of Robinsonades *par excellence*, nonetheless felt compelled to insist that '[*p*] *roduction in general* is an abstraction, but a rational abstraction in so far as it really brings out and fixes the common element.'[90]

General abstractions, abstract universals, transhistorical problematics – or whatever else we wish to call them – find hereby an indispensable role, however prone to misunderstanding, in the construction of social explanations.

We may now return to the stand-off between Walker and Donelan which we left unresolved some pages back. We now know that not one, but two major pitfalls can be identified in the methodological terrain they must each traverse *en route* to their different conclusions. Walker implicitly accuses Donelan and his ilk of falling into the first of these. And he has a point. Timeless truths have long held a special place in IR theory, and the historically specific forms of power at work in the contemporary international system have been correspondingly under-analysed. Donelan's account, whatever its virtues, is certainly one by which (taken on its own) 'no real historical stage of [geopolitical development] can be grasped.' The moment it attempts the latter, it must become (if it is not already) a full-blown Robinsonade.

The question is, however: has Walker succeeded in avoiding the second pitfall – the illicit collapsing of the general into the particular? As we have already seen, he certainly dismisses any notion of a transhistorical problematic of the international; he denies any significant admixture of general determinations in the forms or dynamics of contemporary international relations; and he proposes to derive the latter in their entirety from the unique 'spatio-temporal resolution' of sovereignty as an historically specific political form. These claims are not some disposable wrapping of his argument: they are its very core. They are in fact the only things that distinguish it from the conventional positions of IR theory. And they appear to show him beating a path straight towards our second pitfall, which we might call the pitfall of the inverted Robinsonade.

Before he gets there, however, we have some work of our own to do. For Marx's methodological discussion puts us on the spot too. Our use of it to criticise Walker presupposes the answer to what must now become the key question: can 'the international in general' be a 'rational abstraction'?

Can *every* phenomenon be the object of a 'rational abstraction'? If not, on what grounds can we in fact talk about a problematic of 'the international in general'? And what do we mean by this term 'problematic'? If we cannot provide plausible answers to these questions, Walker's progress across that part of the terrain called IR theory will be smooth indeed. For the pitfall of the inverted Robinsonade will not exist.

Well, we should relax a little. 'Rational abstraction' sounds highly demanding. Fortunately, perhaps, Marx nowhere elaborated a detailed technical procedure which we are compelled to follow in order to produce such a thing. And in other translations, 'rational' is more yieldingly rendered as 'reasonable'. We are free, in other words, to provide our own ordinary-language answers to these questions, using Marx's method as we have already set it out. So let us try to line up the crosshairs of that method on the question of the international.

We shall begin by positioning the second of those hairs – the synchronic conjunction/differentiation of the general and the particular. Is it possible, then, to identify within the totality of human social existence in general a particular dimension which could be referred to as 'the international'? The conventional answer to this question is affirmative: 'international' refers specifically to those aspects of social life which extend (or obtain) across, between and among political communities. Are these aspects susceptible to analysis purely in their own terms? By no means – for they remain 'distinctions within a unity', expressing in their particular domain of social life (the international) determinations characteristic of a given historical form of that life. Do they nonetheless raise questions – political, moral, intellectual – which are not straightforwardly reducible to those encountered in other dimensions of that same given social world? They certainly appear to do so: questions about the political regulation of ungoverned interaction, about the different moral standing of insiders and outsiders, about the intellectual framework necessary to explain the causal dynamics of this 'external' sphere of social life and its relation to the other spheres. Do the answers to these questions (which make up the 'problematic of the international') yield any general determinations, any 'common characteristics' of the international which will therefore 'belong to all epochs'?[91] Maybe. We must look and see. We must complete the crosshair by interpolating into our problematic of the international the diachronic element of Marx's method of abstraction.

And here we immediately encounter a problem. As soon as we step out of the modern world of sovereign states, the word 'international' appears to lose its empirical referent. The fixed borders of sovereign states disappear in a welter of shifting, overlapping jurisdictions. The clear definition of political community dissolves into wider cultural systems, agglomerates into complex, imperial hierarchies, or fragments into roving kinship bands of no fixed territorial definition. One would need a steady nerve – or a reckless disposition – to utter the word 'international' in the face of this menagerie of historical forms.

Yet, in one respect at least, the problem is not dissimilar to that faced by Marx himself in formulating his 'reasonable' abstraction of 'production in general'. For there too the institutionally differentiated form ('the economy') which production assumes in modern capitalist societies is not replicated in premodern societies. There, by contrast, production (like 'the political') is bound up with and organised through all manner of other social relationships, including kinship, gender, caste, political servitude of varying degrees and types – sometimes even, according to Marx himself, language.[92] Did that entail that Marx's abstraction could find no purchase in these cases? No. It rather meant that the object of the abstraction was constituted differently in different historical instances. The lines demarcating its specificity within the wider social order would run differently, and the shape of its presence within that order would vary correspondingly. In each case, therefore, the abstraction, to be applied, would have to take account of this and identify *empirically* the different forms. That, after all, is the whole point of the diachronic element of the method. It is a continuing dialogue between the theoretical abstraction and the concrete historical variation, as a result of which the abstraction is progressively emptied of all but the most general determinations, freeing it of the substantive assumptions which inevitably, but invisibly, attend its initial formulation. And indeed, without this the significance of the historically specific cannot be revealed and analysed.

It would be nice if we could now say the same for our own developing abstraction of 'the international'. But can we? Do we not find, just at this point, a crucial difference which threatens to derail our efforts? To claim that every society engages in production is *obviously* valid. 'Every child knows', Marx famously wrote in a letter to Kugelmann, 'that a country which ceased to work, I will not say for a year, but for a few weeks, would die.'[93] Consequently, to propound a general abstraction of 'production' for the purpose of exploring the different ways in which different societies accomplish this universal necessity seems intrinsically 'reasonable'. And the wider the empirical variation of forms, the greater the value of the general abstraction. Its object will always be found, in some form or another.

No such obviousness attaches to the idea of 'the international in general'. Its object, so easy to fix synchronically in an epoch of sovereign states, seems, once its modern form is stripped away, not to have a wider, general existence. In European feudalism – to confront, as we must, the really hard case – where exactly *was* the line which, by dividing internal from external, makes the synchronic definition of the international conceivable? Did it run between the jurisdictions of individual lordships? Was it defined instead by the reach of the rival kingships to which these lordships might in fealty be bound? Or was it marked by the boundaries of Christendom itself? Each of these has its inside and outside. Which are we to choose? Indeed, since jurisdictions could overlap, fealty could take many forms, and the boundaries of

Christendom were themselves not fixed borders, why should we expect to be able to resolve any of these insides and outsides around the unitary metaphor of a single line at all? And if we cannot, have we not lost the most basic of the 'general determinations' which our prospective category requires?

There is, it must be acknowledged, real force to this criticism. Yet it is arguably a criticism which points to the incompleteness of the exercise, rather than to its intrinsic unreasonableness. In our opening synchronic definition of the international, we allowed a crucial concept to lurk, unproblematised and untheorised, at the very base of the abstraction: the concept of 'political community'. We now discover the hard way what perhaps we should have noticed at the time: a successful general abstraction of 'the international' presupposes a prior general abstraction of 'the political'. For if our conception of 'political community' has not itself first been emptied of its specifically modern attributes, then these will be carried invisibly into our definition of 'the international in general'. And they will indeed render the past unrecognizable. It is this unfinished business which, in the necessary dialogue between theory and history, has now caught up with us. If we want that dialogue to continue, we must take the next step in the process of concept formation: we must release the abstraction for wider historical use by emptying it of the surreptitious modern content which lingers in that pivotal idea of 'political community'.

Needless to say, it would be better if we could abandon the word 'international' too at this point, so redolent is it (unlike 'production') of specifically modern determinations. Alas, the available alternatives – such as geopolitical or intersocietal – bring their own equivalent problems. And in any case, real theoretical problems are not solved by renaming them, and the word 'international' has this virtue: it certainly keeps the problem squarely in our sight. Rather than blight the language with neologisms therefore, let us work instead to evacuate the familiar term.

How are we to conduct the next step? Clearly, the modern assumption which has found its way into our abstraction is a definition of the political as a socially encompassing and territorially unified feature of human collectivities. No reader of Marx's early writings on the state should have let that one slip through the net. Still: how to get rid of it? For this assumption on its own would be sufficient to explain why our derivative abstraction of 'the international in general' could find no purchase in the social world of Christendom. Perhaps the way to proceed is to search for a formulation of 'the political' which supports an equivalent statement to that made by Marx about production in his letter to Kugelmann. (And we might suggest in passing that this is perhaps the test which distinguishes what can from what cannot be the object of a general abstraction. Thus in the current example, if we succeed, we might infer that 'the political' and even 'the international' could qualify, while 'the state' and 'the states-system' would not.) Can we find such a formulation – a definition of the political which does not presuppose its modern form?

Let us say, for example: the political dimension of any social order comprises the means which it has developed (whatever they may be) for arriving at, and giving effect to, collectively binding decisions and rules.[94] Now, does this formulation analytically differentiate a particular aspect of social life from social reproduction in general – does it, in Marx's terms, identify a distinction within a unity? It clearly does. Does it, on its own, enable us to grasp any actual historical form of the political? Certainly not. It is a guide for investigating empirical reality, and only through that investigation of exactly how the political is constituted in given cases can historically specific categories for explaining political processes be generated. It is, in short, an abstraction. Do we know of – or can we even imagine – any human society in which the political dimension as we have formulated it does not exist? If not (and surely the answer is negative), then we have an abstraction which applies universally and transhistorically: we have a general abstraction.

This formulation of 'the political' no longer presupposes, even surreptitiously, the modern, statist definition of politics. It can be used equally, though of course with very different results, to interrogate all manner of social worlds – tribal networks, tributary empires, nation-states – even medieval feudalism. The question is: how does this help us with our main task – the construction of an equivalent general abstraction of 'the international'? If our earlier diagnosis of the problem was correct, the answer should be that this reworking of 'the political' has finally released our abstraction of 'the international' from the tangle of anachronism in which it was still caught. *Everything* now hangs on whether, once so released, the idea of the international retains any determinate analytical content at all. Let us look and see.

When we earlier attempted to define 'the problematic of the international', we identified three constitutive elements which we claimed were irreducible: the political regulation of ungoverned interaction, the differentiated moral standing of insiders and outsiders, and the intellectual (and philosophical) issue of the whole made up by the parts. Was this too just the secret reflex within our reasoning of unpurged modernist assumptions? Or does it still hold, on the basis of our reformulated category of 'the political'? Well, given that no social order has ever yet been coextensive with humanity as a whole, it certainly follows that the collectively binding rules we would identify have always had a limited remit in terms of who is bound by them. This means too that there will always be an inside and an outside; and if the binding rules of political association specify rights and obligations, then how could the moral standing of insiders and outsiders not differ? Moreover, if the collectively binding rules are what demarcate the inside, how could these be the same as the (causal, moral, legal) rules of interaction among these insides (of which, it follows from their non-universal character, there must be more than one)? And if they are not, then the question of the interrelation of these, and of the parts to the superordinate whole, arises also as a *general* question which must be answered in each instance.

We have made an enormous empirical assumption here, it is true. It is an assumption which, in the literature of International Relations, usually arrives heavily loaded with religio-philosophical or social scientific claims. The Christian Pessimists – strongly represented among twentieth-century realists – call it the 'fragmentation' of humankind and trace it mystically back to the biblical Fall of Man.[95] The social scientists call it 'anarchy' and use it to construct an ahistorical, rational-choice model of geopolitical behaviour.[96] Each of these raises hackles and provokes endless attempts at refutation and disproof. Fortunately, we do not need these loadings for our general abstraction of the international to be a reasonable one. We need only the empirical assumption itself: in the known field of human history, social orders have always *co*-existed. Does anybody really want to argue with that?

If not, then we have completed our construction of the international as a 'reasonable abstraction' which can be used in social and historical explanation. Its intellectual standing is no more – but also no less – than that claimed by Marx for his category of 'production in general'. It explains nothing by itself, yet without it, without recognising the general determinations which it captures, no historically specific form of what it abstractly describes can be properly understood either.[97]

And we can now at last unfold the implications of this long methodological discussion for our wider argument. These implications are of three kinds, relating successively to international theory, to the position staked out by Rob Walker, and to the wider claims of globalisation theory.

The implications for international theory lie in the 'general determinations' of the international, and what to do with them. A general determination, following Marx, is one which is indeed 'common to all epochs', yet with which 'no real historical stage . . . can be grasped'. It therefore tells us much and little at the same time. And this in turn helps to explain how realism as a theory can be at once so near to and yet so far from providing an adequate account of world politics.

Realism is right to insist that there is something irreducible, both practically and intellectually, in the nature of international relations. It is right also to observe that this irreducible something has an historical generality which recurs in different forms in different times and places. All societies, in their interactions with others, must provide answers to questions which, at their broadest, have a common form deriving from the general fact of geopolitical co-existence. And there is even a real wisdom to be gained from reflecting on the different answers which have been returned as if they made up a transhistorical canon of international thought; for this indeed helps us both to sift out what is (diachronically) general to the international, and to fix what is particular to it as a distinction within the (synchronic) unity of social reproduction as a whole. For all these reasons, '[t]o say that IR should be reconstituted as a social science does not entail that it either should or would disappear into sociology.'[98]

Realism is wrong, however, whenever it attempts to assemble these general determinations into a free-standing explanatory theory which can be applied in an unmediated way to the real world of international politics. And it is doubly wrong when it tries to buttress that attempt with ahistorical arguments derived either from human nature or from the nature of social science. For *history* is what general determinations most need in order to be safely applied at all. '[T]his explanation is worth nothing', wrote Marx of a general abstraction misused in this way, 'because the historical element is missing from it.'[99] The general determination tells us what to look for in the real historical world; only the historically specific forms of its object can provide the actual basis of explanation. In neorealism, the general determinations of the international have instead been 'hammered out into flat tautologies'.

Nonetheless, the implication for critical international theory still stands: like it or not, there is no way beyond realism by going around it. For, however misconceived it may be, it is sitting on the intellectual foundations (the general determinations) which we too need to make sense of international relations. If the general abstraction holds, then no amount of transnational relations, however powerful, will abolish the analytical moment of the international. And this is why the idea of an outright *replacement* of the problematic of the international by that of globalisation, or global political economy, or world society is ultimately incoherent. (We might even review with some scepticism Marx's own blithe announcement in a footnote to Volume I of *Capital* that 'in order to examine the object of our investigation in its integrity, free from all disturbing subsidiary circumstances, we must treat the whole world of trade as one nation.'[100])

If these implications follow, then the methodological pitfall which we discussed earlier – the pitfall of the inverted Robinsonade – indeed exists. The excessive collapsing of the general into the particular will be as hazardous as the illicit universalising of the particular into the general. What, in Walker's case, will be its intellectual effects?

If the general determinations of the international are not recognised, then their consequences (which after all cannot be wished away) must instead be derived exclusively from what is historically specific. And this perhaps explains what is really holding the theoretical prioritising of space so firmly at the centre of Walker's argument. For it is only by inflating the significance of space beyond that of any other aspect of social life that an alternative source for the effects of those general determinations can be produced. So long as we do not look too closely at other historical worlds (where the general determinations will also be manifest), and so long as we do not question the overall intellectual appropriateness of foregrounding space rather than anything else, then there is indeed a certain inner logic to Walker's argument. Absolute conceptions of space in early modern Europe lead to a spatial definition of politics; the spatial definition of politics renders absolute the severance of inside and outside; the absolute severance of inside and outside underlies the definition and the intractability of the international. And lo: the Robinsonade of 'fragmentation' has been vanquished by the all-conquering principle of historical specificity. The trouble is, not all general abstractions are Robinsonades needing to be cut down. And the price of this victory is in any case too high.

It is too high for us because without those general determinations of 'the international' we will no more be able to make sense of other historical worlds (let alone our own) than if we had been forced down the other road, the denial of what was historically particular to them.

An example of the problems which arise when this simple point is denied may be found in chapter 3 of *Inside/Outside*. There a discussion of the Greek *polis* is used to underline the historical specificity of modern sovereignty by illustrating the very different content that inside and outside may assume when not subjected to an absolute spatial definition. It is in fact a curiously inconclusive discussion. For the first paragraph offers no less than six 'parallels between classical political theory and the principle of state sovereignty'.[101] The second, however, invoking 'the perils of anachronistic interpretation', pushes the other way, arguing that the 'construction of the outsider, of the Other as a radical negation of the Same, is by no means as clear cut' as in the modern case. This counterposition of what is common with what is particular is of course perfectly reasonable – even if Walker manages somehow to avoid mentioning the role of slavery in the Greek *polis*. (That role is especially relevant here because the absolute ban on the enslavement of citizens 'inside' did not generally extend 'outside' to citizens of other *poleis* captured in war. How much more 'clear cut' could a geopolitically defined construction of the outsider become – and that *within* a shared civilisation which held all Greeks to face a common barbarian 'outside', beyond their own city-state system?[102])

But the real problem with Walker's counterpositioning of common and particular features here is that the local use of this procedure surely undermines the wider argument which it is supposed to be illustrating. He can't have it both ways. Either the general determinations which are apparently acknowledged in the first paragraph must also be allowed in the case of modern sovereignty – in which case the spatial derivation of the modern international must be heavily diluted. Or the general determinations, which we earlier derived from the abstraction of the international, need an empirical refutation – and the role of slavery in the Greek *polis* makes the latter an unlikely candidate for that. The simple recognition of different historical forms is, as we saw earlier, no refutation of general abstractions at all.

But if the price is too high for us, we may make so bold as to add that it is perhaps also too high for Walker himself. For here also surely lies the real source of that sense of 'difficulty' which is such an overwhelming rhetorical feature of his writing. If, in his analysis of the modern international system, Walker has in fact conflated an abstract universal with a concrete historical particular, then his repeated claim that imagining a future beyond that system is 'exceptionally difficult' is, if anything, an understatement. For thinking beyond abstract universals is not just difficult: it is a logical impossibility.

Still, the same conflation which makes the further progress of Walker's argument impossible simultaneously explains its appeal to globalisation theory. It may rest on a rudimentary error; but this is an error whose primary effect is a reification of space which is so intense that it magnifies the significance of temporal acceleration and spatial interdependence to earth-shattering intellectual proportions. And here we come finally to the last and greatest irony. For the only way that Walker's argument can now be made to appear on the cutting edge of contemporary thought – rather than ploughing circles in one of its dead ends – is if the claims of globalisation theory should turn out to be empirically substantiated. Perhaps a transformation of space and time really is in the offing which will somehow produce a world in which the problematic of the international dissolves with the historically specific spatio-temporal conditions from which he has sought to derive it. And since he eschews empirical arguments himself, he must rely on those who will make them for him. The circle is therefore now complete. The globalisation theorists who turn to Walker's work for a philosophical backstop to their empirical labours will discover a philosophical argument to be sure – but one which is itself already hanging on for dear life to the empirical backstop, such as it is, of globalisation theory. Which will give way first? It makes little difference. Whichever edge we slide off at this point, our intellectual direction must be downwards, away from the encounter between IR and globalisation theory, and into social theory 'proper', where the foundations of the latter will now be re-laid, using sociological materials, by Anthony Giddens.

4

Giddens' *Consequences of Modernity*: Sociological Foundations?

Introduction

For many of the proponents of globalisation theory, the work of Anthony Giddens, and in particular *The Consequences of Modernity*, has been a key reference point. And this is perhaps not difficult to explain: Giddens has surely done as much as any contemporary thinker to provide an underlying foundation in sociological theory to support the often more partial constructions of globalisation theory. Indeed, by 1990, the elaboration of an alternative, spatio-temporal problematic for social theory was already much more than a *desideratum* in his writings. For some time it had been a developing feature of them; and the outcome – the problematic of time-space distantiation – was now sufficiently developed to allow the category of 'globalisation' to be slotted in at the apex, simultaneously crowning and drawing intellectual respectability from the labour of many years. Giddens also brought to the critique of classical theory a special authority and confidence, derived in part from his earlier work of serious exposition.[1] Finally, his instinctive positioning of his work on the intellectual high ground of social theory had enabled him to draw together a range of concerns normally cut off from each other by the lower-lying boundaries of disciplinary specialisation: how often, after all, does a book appear which interconnects (as does *The Nation-State and Violence*[2]) the findings of psychoanalytic research with the history of Absolutist state-formation and the political strategies of the 1980s 'new social movements'?[3] Critics might cavil at the lightness with which he darted in and out of one specialist literature after another. But an undeniable result was that his own work also became progressively more accessible to a wider and wider intellectual constituency – in a way unmatched by any other writer on globalisation.

Thus Roland Robertson's work on the subject, albeit pioneering in many ways, is less clear-cut than Giddens' in its theoretical implications, partly because it is more ruminative than intellectually programmatic in its tone.[4] Martin Albrow's contribution, by contrast, is probably even more ambitious than Giddens' – but it is also, alas, considerably less comprehensible.[5] The recent volume by David Held et al. – though hailed by James Rosenau as 'the definitive work on globalization' – remains in fact largely descriptive and, in any case, identifies its own theoretical position closely with that of Giddens.[6] Other contributions in IR have tended, as we have seen, to pivot around the traditional preoccupation with the fate of state sovereignty and therefore lack an equivalent currency in the wider social sciences. Meanwhile, Zygmunt Bauman's intervention in the debate, though spirited, has thus far been derivative and impressionistic. Only in Giddens' work then do we find that combination of cumulative theoretical purpose, genuinely interdisciplinary range and unrivalled lucidity of expression which allows us to take the argument at full strength. Not for nothing has *The Consequences of Modernity* functioned so widely as the ur-text of globalisation as a social theory.

For this reason, we shall complete our interrogation of globalisation theory in general via a detailed critical analysis of Giddens' argument in this book. And it may therefore help to provide at this point a brief overview of the key points to follow.

Insofar as it relates to our concerns,[7] the argument of *The Consequences of Modernity* comprises four main steps. The starting point is the claim that we live today in a period of 'high modernity' – a social world which could not have been foreseen by the classical social theorists of the nineteenth and the early twentieth century. The consequent limitations of their analysis of modernity then provides the warrant for the second part of the argument: the suggestion that the classical emphasis upon the analysis of 'societies' should now be replaced by a problematic of 'time-space distantiation' – an attempt to explain social phenomena in terms of how 'social systems' differently organise (and stretch themselves across) the dimensions of space and time. It is this claim, the necessary foundation of globalisation theory, whose validation is next attempted in the third part of the argument, to which most of the book is devoted. Here the alternative problematic is applied directly to the 'globalising' social world of modernity, in which the constitution of the intimate self is argued to be increasingly interwoven with and reconstituted by social processes of a worldwide reach. Finally, Giddens turns to the practical implications of his reinterpretation of modernity for any progressive politics – linking a doctrine of 'utopian realism' with the creative agency of the 'new social movements' in order to imagine what the contours of a genuinely postmodern world might be.

Having said that, however, we shall see that the analytical discreteness of these four steps – a discreteness which must be there if the argument is to be clarified – is not maintained in the progress of the book itself. Above all, steps two and three – the formulation of the alternative problematic and its (logically) subsequent application – are not clearly differentiated. Rather, elements of each alternate with one another across successive chapters, weaving back and forth in ways which make the core of the argument difficult to pin down. Difficult, but not impossible. For gradually it becomes apparent that what is actually going on is quite simple: the further Giddens proceeds with the application of time-space distantiation as an alternative theory, the more this has the effect of emptying the world of recognizably social causes; and this compels him intermittently to make retrospective adjustments to the original 'problematic', in order to re-inject a human content into an analysis otherwise peopled increasingly by impersonal forces and entities which appear to take on a life of their own. Perhaps not surprisingly, this inability of step three to stop fiddling with what should already have been analytically consolidated in step two is replicated in a corresponding failure of either of them to disentangle themselves from materials supposedly discarded in step one. When, for example, Giddens unveils (in chapter 2) his institutional analysis of modernity, it largely comprises a hodge-podge of traditional themes, not a single one of which is defined in spatio-temporal terms.

At both ends, therefore, the new spatio-temporal problematic for social theory turns out to be in a state of continuous and unavoidable implosion. At the 'front', where it extends outwards to construct substantive explanations about the world, these explanations tend to collapse for sheer lack of human social content; meanwhile, at the 'rear', where it is supposed to have detached itself from earlier social theories, categories are sucked into the foundation which undermine its claims to have broken with the past and established a new intellectual discourse.

This predicament, it will be argued, is not a contingent outcome, which can be ascribed to Giddens' failure as an individual theorist. On the contrary, as already implied, he has probably done more than any other writer to give the new problematic what intellectual weight it possesses. The reason lies rather in the fundamental incoherence of the whole idea of a spatio-temporal problematic for social theory – the idea on which, in turn, the wider project of globalisation theory must logically rest. The entire problem would therefore disappear immediately if only writers on the subject reined in their theoretical claims and allowed the term 'globalisation' to resume its original, purely descriptive role. Since, however, this is unlikely to happen, we must stay the course, and try to show in some detail how even the most eminent exponent of globalisation theory, in the book most widely assumed to have provided its underlying foundations, is unable to escape the contradictions which must attend this project at every stage of is construction.

The remaining five sections of this chapter divide the analysis as follows. In 'Making the Break', we shall critically examine Giddens' claim that the globalising world of 'high modernity' requires an intellectual breaking away from the premises of classical social theory. In 'Forward or Back?', we shall ask whether the alternative categories with which he begins the construction of his spatio-temporal problematic do indeed lead us, as he hopes, beyond the limitations of classical theory – or whether in fact they mark a retreat from the latter's deepest insights. In 'Confusion in the Ranks', we record a major instance of the double-ended implosion predicted in the overall diagnosis of the work set out above. The following section, 'The Argument Regroups', describes the most significant of the 'retrospective adjustments' to which the argument is subjected in the course of its exposition – an adjustment which, we shall argue, comes very close to rescuing the work as a whole, and with it the more general foundations of globalisation theory. How that rescue miscarries is the subject of the final section, 'Hide and Seek with Space and Time'. In the concluding chapter, we shall try to explain the overall intellectual collapse which this miscarriage sets in train, together with its implications for globalisation theory in general.

Making the Break

Let us therefore begin at the beginning. '"Modernity"', says Giddens, 'refers to modes of social life or organisation which emerged in Europe from about the seventeenth century onwards and which subsequently became more or less world-wide in their influence.'[8] To this opening place-holder, he immediately attaches two further claims. First, these new modes of social life are so radically different from any historical antecedent that their emergence constitutes a fundamental discontinuity in human history – one whose true scale has conventionally been underestimated due to the predominance of 'social evolutionist' conceptions of historical change. Second, the historical rupture which modernity comprises may be identified descriptively in terms of its effects: an acceleration in the pace of social change (by comparison with premodern societies), a widening of the geographical scope of that change (tending towards a global integration of social relations), and a development of qualitatively unprecedented institutional characteristics of social life. Chief among these latter are the nation-state, industrialism and the commodification of material goods and human services. These institutional forms, in combination with the dynamism and expansiveness of modern modes of life in general, are responsible not only for the material and cognitive advances of the modern period, but also for the equally unprecedented scale and types of danger which contemporary societies face: the potential for totalitarian forms of political rule, the looming threat of environmental disaster, and the ever-present possibility of collective self-destruction through industrialised, and especially nuclear, warfare.

And it is here, in considering this 'double-edged character' of modernity, that Giddens first pauses to spell out systematically the shortcomings of the theoretical legacy bequeathed us by the classical social theories of modernity. The problem, he suggests, is not simply that they failed to 'fully anticipate how extensive the darker side of modernity would turn out to be' [7]. Rather, the very categories we would need in order to understand (or give proper weight to) ecological crisis, totalitarianism and the industrialisation of war are simply not derivable from those earlier theories. And this deficiency in turn he traces to a series of basic assumptions which pervade the work of those classical writers. They are, he suggests, assumptions which the further development of the conditions of modernity has left far behind.

First, both the early theorists and the traditions of thought based upon them today 'have tended to look to a single overriding dynamic of transformation in interpreting the nature of modernity' [11], whether this is identified as capitalism (Marx), industrialism (Durkheim) or rationalisation (Weber). The time has now come, he implies, to end the fruitless competition in which these claims are treated as mutually exclusive: for '[m]odernity, I propose, is *multidimensional on the level of institutions*, and each of the elements specified by these various traditions plays some part' [12].

Second, classical theory and its adherents have, in their very identification of their subject matter, internalised and naturalised a key feature of modernity which needs instead to be exposed and problematised: the definition of sociology as 'the study of societies' presupposes a territorial boundedness of social systems which is both historically peculiar to the modern nation-state, and even then importantly misleading insofar as it tends to ignore important social systems which cross-cut the political boundaries of modern states.

Finally, Giddens criticises classical social theory for failing to understand the significance of its own inescapable involvement in the reflexivity of social knowledge. The Enlightenment belief that greater knowledge of the social world could straightforwardly translate into enhanced self-control of human history has proved illusory precisely because of the scientific form and constitutive role assumed by knowledge in modern social reproduction. The first of these removes the possibility of philosophically grounded certainty and renders all knowledge provisional. The second, meanwhile, installs this inherently unstable, dynamic form of knowledge as the central organising principle of modern societies.

The 'break away from existing sociological perspectives' [16] which Giddens then proposes is indeed a fundamental one. Forms of human social life, he argues, should be investigated not primarily by identifying the material relationships or belief-systems associated with them. Rather, analysis should proceed by specifying in what ways these 'social systems' '"bind" time and space' [14] both quantitatively (meaning how far they stretch social relations across these two dimensions) and qualitatively (meaning how the variety of social systems organise time and space 'so as to connect presence and absence'). Replacing 'societies' with 'social systems' will release social inquiry from the focus on 'bounded entities', making it possible to visualise modern social relations which now extend over much larger tracts of space and time; simultaneously, refocusing on space and time will reveal the truly profound discontinuity which marks off the modern world. This then is the general theory of 'time-space distantiation', which Giddens has been advocating since the 1970s. And, as we already know, it is the logical premise of globalisation theory.

Before examining how Giddens proceeds to implement his proposed shift of problematic, we should pause for a moment to inspect more closely his criticisms of classical social theory. For he seems himself to feel that the constructive argument to follow depends in some crucial way on this prior critique of the classics. And he has therefore returned again and again to this critique over the last twenty years, each time using it as the 'springboard'[9] from which to re-launch his argument in a more developed form. It therefore matters that the springboard should be intellectually secure. But is it?

Five main rivets hold it in place: the charge of social evolutionism, the underestimation of the 'double-edged' character of modernity, the reliance on an institutionally unidimensional basis of explanation, the naturalising of society as a territorially bounded entity, and the indulgence of 'providential outlooks' resting on a failure to grasp the significance of the 'reflexivity' of modernity. Let us consider each of these in turn.

First, then, is it plausible to suggest that, under the influence of an underlying 'social evolutionism', Marx underestimated the radical nature of the transition to modernity by comparison with other transitions in history? Hardly: on the contrary, so convinced was Marx of the enormity of this break that in the *Grundrisse*, as we saw earlier, the entire range of human societies that have existed is collapsed into just two categories: the premodern (organised through 'relations of personal dependence') and the modern (organised through 'personal independence based on *objective* dependence').[10] Consequently, he has been more commonly charged with the opposite error – that of operating with too monolithic a conception of 'premodern' societies.[11] But this point applies more generally. The intellectual axis of Durkheim's social theory, which turns on the distinction between mechanical and organic forms of society, can only apply to the transition to modernity, and must therefore automatically put all other historical transitions into the shade. As for Max Weber, his entire comparative sociology of the world religions is, by his own account, ultimately unable to know non-Western cultures in their own terms: its whole function is to throw into comparative relief just one culture, that of the modern West. The point should not require labouring further: far from being dissolved in the stream of social evolutionism, the radical discontinuity of the modern world was the explicit, self-confessed obsession of classical social theory.[12]

Something similar applies to the second rivet: Giddens' claim that modernity has turned out to be a 'double-edged phenomenon' [7] in ways that require a fundamental revision of the classics. To make such a claim about Marx is really quite extraordinary. For the idea of an inner duality (or, more properly, contradiction) at the heart of modern experience was probably the most familiar and oft-repeated trope in his whole work. Forms of freedom which are also unfreedoms, production of wealth which is simultaneously the production of poverty, and, above all, a fantastic augmentation of human powers which goes along with a collective loss of control by people over the course of their development – all these paradoxes lie at the heart of Marx's analysis of modernity. As Marshall Berman puts it: 'The basic fact of modern life, as Marx experiences it, is that this life is radically contradictory at its base.'[13] And once again, the case can be widened. For Berman suggests that this perception of contradiction is what marks off classical social theory as a whole from later traditions which have embraced either the positive or negative poles:

> Our nineteenth-century thinkers were simultaneously enthusiasts and enemies of modern life, wrestling inexhaustibly with its ambiguities and contradictions; their self-ironies and inner tensions were a primary source of their creative power. Their twentieth-century successors have lurched far more toward rigid polarities and flat totalizations.[14]

Giddens' third rivet appears at first to be sunk into much firmer ground. This is his claim that the classical theorists sought to understand modernity in terms of 'a single overriding dynamic of transformation' [11] such as capitalism, rationalisation or industrialism. 'Modernity', we have seen him assert, 'is *multidimensional on the level of institutions*' [12]. Yet this deceptively bold statement of causal pluralism is in fact capable of doing much less work than its textual italicization suggests. Let us look into it for a moment.

The first point to note is that this very claim is already built into the understandings of modernity provided by both Marx and Weber. For Marx, as Giddens himself later notes in passing [56], the differentiation of politics and economics *on the level of institutions* is central to the very definition of capitalist society. And for Weber, it is precisely the increasing institutional 'differentiation of spheres' and their mutual irreconcilability which comprises the major outcome of rationalisation as an historical and cultural process. Thus it is logically false to counterpose institutional multidimensionality to any 'single overriding dynamic' – unless of course one begins with a definition of capitalism or rationalisation as institutionally unidimensional. In that case, however, the resultant criticism cannot (for the reasons just given) be levelled at classical social theory.

Second, however, Giddens' qualifier – 'on the level of institutions' – implicitly leaves open the possibility that modernity might indeed be unidimensional at some other, deeper level. At the very least, it suggests that part of any account of how the various institutional dimensions of modernity are interrelated might have to be an explanation of why, uniquely in modernity, they have become differentiated in this way to begin with.

In any case, if Giddens interprets modernity as being made up of a plurality of mutually irreducible institutional forms, this interpretation cannot in itself be a reason for breaking with the classical tradition. For pluralism of this kind is exactly what, taken collectively, it already provides, with each writer emphasising a different institutional element. If, therefore, one proclaims a break with the tradition as a whole, the reason is just as likely to be a desire to reimpose some overarching order by introducing a new 'single, overriding dynamic of transformation'.

And one has to ask whether time-space distantiation does not come increasingly to play this role in Giddens' account – and if so, how it compares with the existing Marxian and Weberian alternatives.

This leaves only two rivets holding the springboard in place: the claim that the classics reified the historically transient experience of the nation-state into an underlying conception of society as a territorially bounded entity; and the further charge of the classics' inattention to the special reflexivity of knowledge under conditions of modernity.

Now, it is truly difficult to see how the first of these could find any real purchase in the work of Marx. Is this not the same Marx whose break with Hegel pivoted around the latter's dehistoricising and fetishising of the modern state, who insisted in 1844 that, 'above all, we must avoid reifying "society"', and who followed this up in the *Communist Manifesto* of 1848 by declaring that bounded entities were no more? In fact, Marx was so far from such a position that, once again, there is more mileage in the opposite charge, namely that he was so unimpressed by bounded entities that he neglected the real historical significance of the nation-state – a charge which indeed Giddens himself, in an earlier volume, had levelled against Marx.[15]

As for the idea that the classical tradition lacks an adequate sense of modern reflexivity, one must wonder what understanding of Weber's writings could possibly sustain such a view.[16] Weber went to considerable lengths to define sociology as a 'cultural science'[17] – concerned with understanding how different worldviews were expressed in contrasted institutional forms, forms which in turn governed not only the contexts of action but also the ways in which human existence could be experienced as meaningful. And within this general affirmation of the reflexivity of social knowledge, the impact of 'the specific and peculiar Western form of rationalism' formed *the central object* of his entire comparative sociology of the world-religions. For it was precisely in the further spin which this cultural development gave to the circularity of social knowledge that Weber saw the momentum for both the uncontrollable spread of bureaucratic and calculative forms of action and the rise of the 'scientific' worldview – together with their corresponding subjective attributes of the depersonalising of social processes and the ungroundability of metaphysical truths. Thus, Giddens' diagnosis of the Enlightenment – still half-submerged in 'providential outlooks' – would hardly have been news to Max Weber. Indeed, for him, its 'rosy blush' was already 'irretrievably fading'.[18] And far from trying to replace it with new visions of human self-mastery, he was already installing the cultural predicament of the special reflexivity of modern knowledge forms at the very heart of his definition of modernity itself; this, after all, was part of what he meant by the haunting observation that we live in 'an epoch which has eaten of the tree of knowledge'.[19]

Given all this, we should perhaps also question the ease with which Giddens assumes that totalitarianism, the industrialisation of warfare and the emergence of an ecological crisis may safely count as concrete examples of problems lying beyond the analytical reach of the classics. For, as Benedict Anderson has powerfully argued, the naturalising of bureaucratic rationality and its substantive counterposing to charisma (a separation which would indeed render the phenomenon of totalitarianism incomprehensible) was the work not of Weber himself, but rather of the selective and distorting appropriation of Weber's categories by postwar American social science.[20] Similarly, if one wanted to address the ecological crisis, one might well view the productivist mania of Third International Marxism, driven by the ideological requirements of backward industrialisation, as part of the problem and not the solution. But if central to that solution (as Giddens holds) is a conception of 'socialised nature', a humanly transformed environment whose very transformation feeds back in both intended and unintended ways into a kind of dynamic self-creation of humanity as a species – if this is the focus we need, then it is hard to see how the ecological crisis provides an argument against the historical materialism of Marx, whose ontology corresponds exactly and perhaps even uniquely to these *desiderata*.[21]

What explains the remarkable inaccuracy of Giddens' representation of classical social theory – remarkable not least in the light of his own early crusade to rescue that tradition from earlier misrepresentations?[22] We should first rule out of account either intellectual incapacity or scholarly bad faith. Neither of these applies. Perhaps a clue may be found if we notice that Giddens' critique, albeit misdirected here, is by no means bereft of very deserving targets elsewhere. At any rate it seems significant that at various earlier points in his intellectual development, Giddens used a quite different springboard for the theoretical reconstructions whose announcement and reannouncement have characterised his successive publications. At these points is was not classical social theory, but rather an 'orthodox consensus' of postwar American sociology – dominated by the figure of Talcott Parsons – which was accused, *inter alia*, of evolutionism and a failure to grasp the significance of reflexivity for the understanding of social life.[23] Indeed in 1971, in a book which explicitly cites Marx's opposition to social evolutionism as a transhistorical error,[24] Giddens had argued that a return to the classics was a necessary part of any break with this consensus.[25] By 1984, however, when he came to make his formal statement of structuration theory, not only had he reverted to the engagement with the (now dissolved) 'orthodox consensus' as the starting point; in addition, the legacy of the classical writers had itself begun to be absorbed into the object of his critique. The observation that in the postwar period, '[t]hose who regarded themselves as both sociologists and Marxists tended to share the basic assumptions of functionalism and naturalism' was already sliding into the initially guarded but increasingly unargued claim that '"[h]istorical materialism", I think, is a version of evolutionism.'[26]

Thus, it begins to appear as if an initial use of the classics against postwar American sociology passed first into a not unreasonable claim that their latter-day followers had been methodologically absorbed into the 'orthodox consensus', only to end up later with a reading back of elements of this same 'orthodox consensus' into the classics themselves.[27]

By the time of *The Consequences of Modernity*, this intervening intellectual history has once again been submerged, and Giddens appears to be alone with the classics. Yet there is a price to be paid, in the form of a revealing 'return of the repressed'. For by now misdirecting his fire in this way, Giddens not only makes claims about classical social theory which are unsustainable; he also unwittingly lowers his guard against exactly those discourses which should have been the objects of his critique in the first place. Specifically, as his argument develops, the alienated categories of Parsonian systems theory, no longer visibly crossing his sights, emerge as if from behind to colonise his analysis.[28] And this time Giddens is powerless to resist or even perceive this infiltration. For the key to identifying and reversing it lies buried within the classical social theories which he has just begun by discarding.

Having said this, we should remember that these are not Giddens' problems alone. Although for him (as their presence in his earlier, 'pre-globalisation' writings indicates) they are not originally generated by the idea of globalisation, some kind of rejection of the classics is nonetheless arguably inscribed in any attempt to consolidate globalisation theory as a problematic for social theory. For the need to derive explanatory mechanisms within the descriptive features of globalisation must, if worked through, generate claims about the causal significance of space and time which compete directly with the alternative premises of either Marx's 'materialist conception of history' or Weber's 'cultural science'. It is presumably exactly this which Bauman, for example, implies when he writes that '[m]odern history has been marked by the constant progress of the means of transportation'[29] – a choice of words which echoes, surely in order directly to counterpose, Marx's equivalent claim about the means of production.

Forward or Back?

But the time has come to move on to the constructive part of Giddens' argument. Having delivered his critique, where does he now turn in order to start building his alternative problematic?

In line with his earlier methodological proposal, he begins by establishing a descriptive contrast between 'time-space relations' in the modern and the premodern world. In the latter, time and space were inseparable from each other and (or rather because) both were inseparable from the social and natural relations and activities whose movement they choreographed: '"[W]hen" was almost universally either connected with "where" or identified by regular natural occurrences' [17]. And space too was imagined and ordered not by applying an abstract uniform measure, but rather in terms of 'place': concrete sites of social activity. What was missing therefore was the distinctively modern conception of 'empty time', on the one hand, and 'empty space', on the other. For it is the linked emergence of these two conceptions which opened out the spatio-temporal dimensions of human experience into a separately imaginable grid, within which social relations could be freely reorganised, and by which they could be measured and co-ordinated. The necessary historical conditions of this distinctively modern time-space were provided by the early modern Discoveries and the industrial revolution. The first promoted the cartographic attempt to represent the distribution and shape of the world's regions according to the abstract, geometrical divisions of global space itself (longitude and latitude); and the later diffusion of clocks and watches among whole populations during the industrial revolution established a temporal framework potentially independent of any events occurring within it.

The resultant separation of space from time is, Giddens argues, 'crucial to the extreme dynamism of modernity' [20] in three ways. First, the ability which it creates to co-ordinate social relations and activities precisely over large stretches of space and time becomes the precondition for that process of 'disembedding' which 'lifts' social relations out of purely local contexts and reconnects them to wider structures of indefinite geographical scope – it is, as will later appear, the ultimate precondition for 'globalisation'. Second, this same separation of space and time underpins the existence of the dominant form of human agency which orchestrates and moves within this new

medium – 'the rationalised organisation' [20]. Bureaucratic plan-
ning, after all, depends upon the predictable ordering of persons
and things in particular spatio-temporal configurations – timetables,
work-routines, and so on. Finally, once time has been abstracted from
place and re-imagined as uniform, linear and empty, it enables not
only the opening up of the future to calculative manipulation, but
also 'the appropriation of a unitary past' as 'history' [21] – 'empty
time' thus underpins 'the radical historicity associated with modernity' [20].

What, then, produces and sustains the 'disembedding' of social
relations which lies at the heart of this process? At this stage in the
argument, Giddens identifies two objective mechanisms – 'symbolic
tokens' and 'expert systems' – and one subjective orientation: 'trust'.

Symbolic tokens are defined as 'media of interchange which can be
"passed around" without regard to the specific characteristics of individuals or groups that handle them at any particular juncture' [22].
Such a definition points most clearly to the case of money. And
although he implies, without explaining, the existence of other symbolic tokens ('such as media of political legitimacy'), it is indeed
money which Giddens chooses to illustrate his argument. 'What is
money?' [23] he asks. And his answer is as follows. Money, in both its
early and most developed forms, is essentially debt (and hence simultaneously credit). It is a symbol of material obligation interposed
within the process of exchanging things which arrests the process
halfway, and thus allows its completion to be deferred in time and
space. Direct barter first gives way to 'commodity money', then to written IOUs backed by banking organisations, next to state-regulated
national currencies, and finally to 'pure information lodged as figures in a computer printout' [25]. But throughout this process of
development, the defining property is constant: by embodying material obligation in quantifiable form, money releases the process of
exchange from the spatio-temporal constraints of barter and allows it
to be stretched indefinitely across space and time. It disembeds the
process of exchange.

Expert systems also release social relations from confinement in local space and time, but their focus is wider than that of material exchange. Expert systems are defined as 'systems of technical accomplishment or professional expertise that organise large areas of the material and social environments in which we live today' [27]. More specifically, they comprise bodies of specialised knowledge – ranging from codes of law to natural scientific research – together with the organisations through which that knowledge is involved in the organisation of the natural and social worlds. Their importance is revealed when we consider just how far the constructed environments in which members of modern societies exist are 'thoroughly permeated by expert knowledge' [28]. Routine activities such as switching on a light or driving a car involve individuals in dependence upon depersonalised structures of scientific knowledge and social regulation which extend far beyond either their immediate physical experience or indeed their mental awareness. Viewed the other way about, expert systems regulate local events and personal interactions, while being themselves abstracted from locality, and regulated by impersonal criteria.

Given this propensity of disembedding to generate a routine dependence on structures of knowledge and interaction which are, from the point of view of any individual, both uncontrollable and even unknowable, it is understandable that Giddens should be interested also in exploring the subjective dimension of the disembedded world of modernity. This brings us to his discussion of 'trust'. He uses the term to indicate a highly specific phenomenon. Trust, in this context, is a psychological precipitate of the secularised ontology of modernity. The decline in the belief in divinely or naturally ordained causes as the basis of social explanation, together with the increased awareness of how much of the social and even natural environment is reproduced through the operation of increasingly complex expert systems – these combine to transform the kinds of contingency which human beings must face in their lives. And this transformation is reflected in a corresponding shift in the subjective form in which that contingency is apprehended: the increasing displacement of 'fortuna' by 'risk'. Increasingly, challenges faced by individuals are known to be the outcomes – intended or otherwise – of human systems and actions. And confidence in the reliability of the external world now takes the form of a faith – trust – in the abstract principles embodied in the systems, with consequences to which Giddens returns later in his argument.

At this point, however, we must pause for a moment. We are, it will be recalled, accompanying our author in his elaboration of 'a fresh characterisation of modernity', one which is intended to 'break away' from traditional perspectives. It seems only reasonable, therefore, to take an opportunity for a first look back over the ground we have covered so far: how far have we actually travelled from the classical schemas earlier discarded, and in what direction?

Let us consider first the concept of 'symbolic tokens', which Giddens has applied to the analysis of money.

Marx, as is well known, was not silent on the question of money. Indeed, the first three chapters of *Capital* are largely devoted to a deconstruction of 'the magic of money'.[30] The purpose of this deconstruction is to reveal how the apparently innate technical properties of money as a thing – above all its fungibility and role as a unit and store of value – were in fact the emergent properties of a particular kind of human relationship. Marx's fundamental criticism of 'vulgar economy' was that it persistently reified these emergent properties, attributing them to the material objects through which they operated, rather than tracing them back to the generative human relations themselves.

This being the case, it is remarkable that Giddens could take up (let alone attribute to Marx) the view that 'money permits the exchange of anything for anything . . . because of its role as a "pure commodity"' [22]. For this formulation is dangerously close to exactly the fetishism which Marx was attempting to overturn. 'It is', he wrote, 'not money that renders the commodities commensurable. Quite the contrary.' For him, the fungibility of money, far from being the original facilitator of exchange, merely posed in its sharpest form the underlying puzzle of the commodity itself – namely, what is the thing 'value' in terms of which otherwise unlike objects can be equated for exchange, and which seems to find its purest expression in money? Or as he puts it: 'The riddle of the money fetish is therefore the riddle of the commodity fetish, now become visible and dazzling to our eyes.'[31]

The casual reader who does not have time to check the accuracy of Giddens' citations[32] will probably also not be aware that the treatment of money as a 'symbolic token' is one of several approaches to the subject explicitly considered (and rejected) by Marx in chapter 2 of *Capital*. '[I]n this way,' he wrote there, 'the Enlightenment endeavoured, at least temporarily, to remove the appearance of strangeness from the mysterious shapes assumed by human relations whose origins they were unable to decipher.'[33] To describe money as a symbol, he argued, does at least 'contain the suspicion that the money-form of the thing is external to the thing itself'. But it does nothing on its own to uncover the actual sociological referent of money, the 'thing itself' which this symbol represents. And yet without that, all the technical properties of money which render it such a potent phenomenon are immune to sociological inquiry. If anything, this need for a genuinely *social* theory of value should be even more obvious now than in Marx's time. For as Giddens points out, '[t]oday, "money proper" is independent of the means whereby it is represented, taking the form of pure information lodged as figures in a computer printout' [25]. What then is 'it'? Giddens' answer – '[m]oney in its developed form is . . . defined above all in terms of credit and debt' [24] – simply begs the question: credits and debts *of what?*

Now, it is important to be clear about exactly what is at stake in this criticism. The issue is not simply whether Marx or Giddens provides a better technical analysis of money. It concerns rather the overall conception of how deeply the specifically social construction of reality reaches into our experience of the world – and, correspondingly, what the ultimate possibilities and requirements of social theory therefore comprise.

In the case of Marx, much of the intellectual excitement with which the early chapters of *Capital* are aflame clearly derives from a belief that in attempting to answer the question 'what is value?', he had uncovered a layer of social determinations lying far deeper in the constitution of reality than any earlier writer had even thought to delve. For it now turned out that even the apparent objectivity of things as values was the encoded form of a particular historical kind of social relation, waiting to be deciphered by a theory attuned to the critique of objectification as a cultural phenomenon. The direction of Marx's argument is therefore exactly opposite to that attributed to him and then taken up by Giddens: it is not money which, with reference to its innate technical qualities, is used to explain the commodification of social relations; rather the technical qualities of money are revealed as themselves the reified expression of an ontologically prior form of social relation. And although the movement of the 'things' caught up in this relation (i.e. commodities and money) indeed had a technical regularity which could be tracked and systematised in an apparently self-enclosed discourse of 'economics', it now became possible in principle to elaborate an alternative, *sociological* discourse in which the technical characteristics of the things themselves could at last be understood as emergent properties of a particular historical form of human agency.

Thus in elaborating this discourse, Marx not only advanced a specific argument about money; he simultaneously extended the explanatory claims of social theory as a whole. Value theory, in this light, is the argument by which Marx captured the subject matter of 'economics' for social theory. And one can only look on in disbelief as Giddens (by re-reifying money) now proceeds to hand it back without even a struggle, contenting himself instead with the much shallower social ontology implicit in the proto-Parsonian category of 'symbolic tokens'.[34]

For by defining these as 'media of interchange which can be "passed around" without regard to the specific characteristics of individuals or groups' [22], Giddens has *begun* by abstracting symbolic

tokens from both their historical specificity and their sociological constitution. And this is a fatal step. For it is simply not true that money
(or *any* social artefact, for that matter) circulates 'without regard to the
specific characteristics of individuals and groups'. In order for money
to be 'passed around' in the way he describes presupposes at least a
partial commodification of social life, which is precisely a 'specific
characteristic' of some 'groups' and not others. It is at any rate not an
historical universal. To this, Giddens may reply that he is describing
the role and properties of this symbolic token within the historical
context of modernity, that the category is not intended for transhistorical application, and its historical specificity may in this sense be
taken as given. The trouble is that it is exactly the 'given-ness' of social
phenomena which renders them no longer the objects of analysis,
and which in this case seals off the deeper path of sociological inquiry,
thereby allowing the 'consequences' which derive from the remarkable behavioural properties of this 'token' to reappear as non-human,
purely technical phenomena.

It might be argued in defence of Giddens that his purpose here is
not to explain the foundation of money as a social form but rather to
point to its consequences for the disembedding of social relations and
their stretching across space and time: '[M]oney is a means of time-
space distantiation. . . . [It provides] a means of bracketing time-space
by coupling instantaneity and deferral, presence and absence' [24–5].
It thereby also constitutes a crucial condition for the process of globalisation. Once again, however, it would be ludicrous to suppose that
exactly these spatio-temporal implications of developed exchange-rela-
tions were not central also to Marx's account of the process.
'Circulation', he wrote in chapter 3 of *Capital*, 'bursts through all the
temporal, spatial and personal barriers imposed by the direct
exchange of products, and it does this by splitting up the direct identity present in this case between the exchange of one's own product
and the acquisition of someone else's.'[35] The major difference
between Marx's account and that of Giddens is therefore not that
Marx is less attentive to the transformations of time and space

involved. It is rather that instead of attributing them to the technical properties of a thing, he has sought to show in what way they arise as emergent properties of a particular form of social life:

> The more production comes to rest on exchange value, hence on exchange, the more important do the physical conditions of exchange – the means of communication and transport – become for the costs of circulation. Capital by its nature drives beyond every spatial barrier. Thus the creation of the physical conditions of exchange – of the means of communication and transport – the annihilation of space by time – become an extraordinary necessity for it.[36]

And this perhaps is why Marx's analysis, for all its problems, develops seamlessly into an exposition of the power relations among people which are articulated through the movement of things; meanwhile Giddens' account – as we shall see later – builds more and more into a picture with people on the one side and disembodied systems on the other, in which power itself ceases to be an organic category but is replaced by the purely technical variable of 'risk'. Statements made later about unequal power are sourced outwith his central argument, and must be bolted on from the outside. [See p. 154.] And Parsons, who rarely appears in Giddens' writings except as a target of criticism, and who really should have been locked out if Giddens was serious about providing 'a fresh characterisation of modernity', has nonetheless somehow got his foot back in the door right at the start.

Capital is not any easy work to read. But more significantly, its central argument is *so* counter-intuitive that even once it has been understood, it can quickly be lost again, swamped beneath the unending stream of countervailing perceptions which make up the experience of everyday life in capitalist societies. And one does find oneself asking how long it has actually been since Giddens last reread those early chapters.[37]

The argument, however, does not rest on symbolic tokens alone. There are also the 'expert systems'. And this brings us to the vexed question of the relation between Giddens' work and that of Max

Weber. It is vexed because Giddens himself later explicitly recognises that Weber gave special attention to the role of expert systems in characterising modernity. 'Among the three major founders of modern sociology,' he says, 'Weber saw most clearly the significance of expertise in modern social development and used it to outline a phenomenology of modernity' [137–8]. This is certainly true, and it is gracious of Giddens to acknowledge it. But in that case, why are we pursuing a 'fresh characterisation' of modernity? The answer must presumably be that Giddens believes himself able, on the basis of his new theory, to understand something crucial about modernity which cannot be grasped using Weber's categories. We must therefore ask: what is it that Giddens has seen which could not already be seen by Weber? Let us consider the evidence.

It cannot be that Giddens is claiming that 'expert systems' are more unique to, or more dominant within, or more significant for modernity than Weber realised. For Weber's position on these points was already extreme:

> [N]o age has ever experienced, in the same sense as the modern Occident, the absolute and complete dependence of its whole existence, of the political, technical, and economic conditions of its life, on a specially trained *organization* of officials.[38]

Nor could it be claimed that by using the term 'officials', Weber was emphasising state organisations over others. His focus was explicitly on 'expert systems' *per se*. 'It does not matter for the character of bureaucracy whether its authority is called "private" or "public".'[39] But Giddens' category of 'expert systems', it might be said, is about more than the organisational structure of persons in bureaucracies; it also includes the bodies of specialised knowledge – technical, legal, even philosophical – which are mediated to the lay world by experts and which saturate the daily lived experience of modernity. Well, exactly the same could be said of Weber's category of 'rationalisation', a term which includes scientific specialisation understood as the intellectual counterpart of the developing social form of bureaucratic organisation.

Weber also saw that the result of this process of rationalisation was not a new transparency to social life:

> Does it mean that we, today . . . have a greater knowledge of the conditions of life under which we exist than has an American Indian or a Hottentot? Hardly. Unless he is a physicist, one who rides on the streetcar has no idea how the car happened to get into motion.[40]

What it actually meant, he saw, was a new subjective orientation – 'trust'? – based on a belief that in principle the natural and social worlds could be understood by secular means – not least because, as the example of the streetcar illustrates, they were already increasingly under the sway of those means. Weber also saw that this new subjective orientation corresponded to the key institutional forms of modernity – the capitalist market and the legal-rational state. He saw that, behaviourally, the essence of these forms was the pressure that they imposed on individuals to behave in calculatively rational ways – '[E]verything is done in terms of balances . . . calculation underlies every single action . . . exact calculation [becomes] the basis of everything else.'[41] And he saw that these ways of behaving then reflexively become the object of rationalised scientific analysis which itself then feeds back into the reconstitution of the social reality it describes. When, towards the end of his lecture on 'Science as a Vocation', Weber has finished peeling away all the possible social and philosophical roles which rationalised knowledge can no longer play, something very like 'risk analysis'[42] is among the few roles remaining. In fact, Weber even analysed the peculiar interrelation of reflexivity and autopoietic systems, via a discussion of one of Giddens' favourite illustrations of this: the stock market. And he argued that modern social conditions generalised this phenomenon to 'all other spheres of action as well'.[43]

Is Giddens then simply re-inventing Weber? Would that he were. For just as his attempt to go beyond Marx arguably left him far behind, reproducing instead the very reifications which *Capital* began by overturning, so something similar applies here. This classical theorist too has more and deeper things to say about the modern world than anyone would guess from what comes through in *The Consequences of Modernity.*

To gain a sense of what these might be, we must, as with Marx, ask what kind of argument it is which lies at the heart of Weber's *oeuvre.* We may dismiss at the start the most common misperception – that Weber ascribed European 'modernity' to its more rational, or ratio-nalised, character, by contrast with other cultures which remained mired in religion. For rationalisation, he insisted several times, 'is an historical concept which covers a whole world of different things'. And these things may even include 'rationalization of mystical con-templation, that is of an attitude which, viewed from other departments of life, is specifically irrational'. Not rationalism in gen-eral, then, but 'the specific and peculiar rationalism of Western culture' becomes the real object of inquiry: 'It is hence our first con-cern to work out and to explain genetically the special peculiarity of Occidental rationalism, and within this field that of the modern Occidental form.'[44]

The counterposition of reason and religion as opposites – per-haps the single greatest obstacle to understanding what Weber is really up to – is further broken down by a second kind of reading, focused on *The Protestant Ethic and the Spirit of Capitalism.* For here the 'genetic' analysis produces an apparently paradoxical result: the ori-gins of the secularised ontology and epistemology of modernity are traced to a specifically religious development. Or to put it the other way around, the historical world of secularism turns out to have been generated by a particular form of religious belief. But what is the sig-nificance of this? To find out, we must locate the preceding points within a third reading, which takes Weber's comparative sociology of the world-religions as the key orienting focus of his work. For with this move, Western rationalism finally becomes available for analysis, understood not as the opposite of religion, nor simply as a freak his-torical product of religion, but rather as itself a particular and peculiar form of world-religion – meaning a composite of institutional and mental forms defining a particular cultural-historical way of being human.

To rediscover Western 'reason' as a cultural particular in this way – without, moreover, dismissing its epistemological claims[45] – is really quite an achievement. Western rationalism thereby becomes not the historical exit from 'culture', but rather available – like any world-religion – for analysis in terms of the tensions involved in the inner meaning of being human in this particular cultural way. This in turn enables us to get under the skin of an apparently purely technical phenomenon like bureaucracy as an organisational form, and to see it again as the one thing it most appears not to be: human. Flesh-and-blood human beings are back at the core of the attempt to explain the apparently dehumanised, alienated social forms of modernity. Once again, however, the direction of Giddens' analysis reverses us away from the insight of the classical author. By failing to problematise the apparent 'abstraction' of expert systems from historical cultures, he inevitably renaturalises their properties in such a way that their deeper, anthropological interrogation is increasingly sealed off as a basis for explanation. The eventual result of this process becomes fully apparent in chapter 5 of *Consequences*, by which time the broad human question of abstract systems reappears in the purely technical form of 'design faults' and 'operator failure' compounded by 'the circularity of knowledge' [151–3]. Such metaphors, one cannot help but feel, simply reproduce at a cognitive level the reification of human agency built into the cultural form itself – and which it should rather be the purpose of a social theory to demystify and explain. And once again they imply the deep penetration of Parsonian systems theory into the heart of the argument.

As we shall see later, Giddens does also attempt a kind of re-appropriation of the human experience of bureaucracy – but it is a cramped, ethnomethodological one which begins with the form itself already externalised. And this is largely because, just as with the earlier example of 'tokens' (defined as abstracted from social characteristics), an initial failure to problematise the institutional form of bureaucracy establishes a floor on how deeply any subsequent analysis of its meaning and effects can go.

It is true that, taken on its own, Weber's analysis of bureaucracy seems to point to an increasing rigidification of social life, an impression reinforced by grim predictions about 'mechanised petrification', 'iron cloaks' and the rest. But to take it on its own would be to abstract it from the wider analysis of the calculative rationality it promotes – a rationality rooted above all in the *dynamic* properties of the capitalist market which for Weber was the ultimate archetype and driving force of the overall process. And while it is certainly true that Giddens is more optimistic than Weber, this cannot really count as an analytical increment to his argument, because it is based not on a resolution of Weber's concerns but on a simple failure to take them up at all.

Just as with Marx, then, so too with Weber: the range of phenomena which his approach was able to constitute as the object of sociological understanding was wider and richer than Giddens' discourse can encompass. And Giddens' deployment of his category of 'expert systems', by renaturalising bureaucracy, must be seen to involve not an advance on classical theory, but another retreat from one of its profoundest intuitions.

Marx and Weber, however, are not the only classical thinkers to be treated in this way. The problematic nature of Giddens' use of other writers' ideas is a major and even at times an embarrassing feature of the secondary literature.[46] However, since a fuller discussion of this would carry us away from our theme, let us confine ourselves to one further example from *Consequences*, an example which has direct relevance to globalisation theory. The views of Clausewitz, we are told on page 58, 'were already substantially obsolete when he developed them'. As if this extraordinary claim were not enough, Giddens then follows it up by invoking the emergence of total war as evidence – without even mentioning that for not a few writers the conceptual origins of this idea lie in the work of – yes – Clausewitz. By page 75, 'the obsolescence of Clausewitz's main doctrine has become apparent to everyone.' This is so straightforwardly false as a claim about the relevant scholarly fields[47] that one turns urgently to the foot-noted reference on page 183 to find out who this 'everyone' might be, only to find instead a sentence which, far from substantiating the claim, blithely contradicts it: 'Clausewitz was a subtle thinker, however, and there are interpretations of his ideas which continue to insist upon their relevance to the present day.' Subtle? 'This concep-tion [namely 'that war cannot be divorced from political life'] would be ineluctable even if war were total war.'[48] How much plainer could Clausewitz have been?

The evasiveness here is so extreme that one can't help feeling that even Giddens himself might experience some relief if only someone would pin him down and sort out the muddle he has ended up in. It cannot, after all, be very satisfying for someone of Giddens' real intel-ligence to rest with a vulgar reading of Clausewitz which renders the latter's greatest insight inaccessible.

Something should be said about this emerging pattern of misrep-resentation. The social sciences, as Giddens is keen to point out, themselves comprise an abstract system, in which trust is routinely placed in the reliability of 'experts' to report knowledgeably about bodies of thought whose content and justification lie beyond the reach of non-specialists. Among the specialists themselves, this need for 'trust' is displaced by a critical mutual interrogation among equals, facilitated by the scholarly apparatus of detailed referencing. *The Consequences of Modernity* lacks such an apparatus, perhaps legitimately, because although it is addressed to other intellectuals, the vast major-ity of these will be, from the point of view of the specialist studies of individual classical thinkers, lay participants in the system. This means, however, that the pronouncements of this book are largely *ex cathedra*, and therefore demand an unusually high degree of trust. If Giddens wants to write as if Marx had never addressed the disembedding of social relations, the depersonalised form of the market as an abstract system, or even the resultant subjective issue of trust, then of course he should be free to do so.[49] But insofar as his readers trust him to report 'expertly' on the tradition he criticises, it must be said that he renders them a disservice. Strictly speaking, however, this problem is relevant to us only if it appears to derive from intellectual imperatives imposed by the pursuit of a spatio-temporal problematic for social theory. And this would be hard to substantiate in respect of the treatment of Clausewitz. It is more likely to play a role in the displacement of Marx and Weber, and we should keep this in mind as we proceed to the next stage of the argument.

Confusion in the Ranks

Havoc in the Rear

At this point, however, something rather curious happens. We predicted at the start of this chapter that any attempt to consolidate a spatio-temporal problematic for social theory would be prone to an unavoidable implosion at both ends, with its concrete explanations collapsing at the 'front' and its theoretical premises continually being invaded by extraneous concepts at the 'rear'. We have already just seen an anticipation of the former in the discussion of symbolic tokens and abstract systems, and a fuller collapse will follow, as promised, at the start of chapter 3. Before we get there, however, we must work our way through a remarkable illustration of its underlying counterpart: analytical havoc in the rear. The point at which this state of affairs becomes apparent lies exactly where one would expect to find it – in the formulation of the institutional definition of modernity in chapter 2.

In the midst of this formulation, Giddens reiterates the methodological shift which he is trying to effect: 'The undue reliance which sociologists have placed upon the idea of "society", where this means a bounded system, should be replaced by a starting point that concentrates upon analysing how social life is ordered across time and space – the problematic of time-space distantiation' [63–4]. By this stage, however, it is already apparent that this is not what is actually happening – either terminologically, or at the deeper theoretical level where time-space distantiation should be starting to play an explanatory role. Terminologically, the distinction between 'society' and 'social system' rapidly breaks down and is in practice abandoned, leading to a veritable riot of bounded entities. 'Societies', 'states', 'civilisations', 'nations', even 'countries', all merrily elbow their way back onto his pages.[50] More importantly, however, by this point all four of the institutional clusters which flesh out the definition of modernity have been introduced: capitalism, industrialism, surveillance and centralised control of the means of violence. Not one of these is defined in terms of a particular ordering of social life across time and space. On the contrary, several of them – and one in particular – are identified as possessing social attributes which in fact generate the spatio-temporal phenomena which Giddens wishes to foreground as primary.

That one, perhaps not surprisingly, is capitalism. Giddens' definition of capitalism – a class system of commodity production, based on private property and wage labour, and regulated by market mechanisms – is not framed in terms of the binding of space and time. It certainly is shown to have enormous spatio-temporal consequences: it is 'intrinsically unstable and restless' and 'inherently highly dynamic' [61]; and these properties underpin 'expansionist characteristics' which both make it 'only in a few respects confined to the boundaries of specific social systems' [57] and also generate a temporal momentum based on the fact that 'technological innovation tends to be constant and pervasive' [56]. But time-space distantiation is clearly not the starting point here. On the contrary, it is what is being explained by a methodologically prior, materialist theory of capitalism.

Capitalism in fact turns out in these pages to be so significant that it even undermines the causal pluralism which Giddens wishes to install at the centre of his substantive definition of modernity. He sees the latter as a conjunction of the four mutually irreducible 'institutional clusterings' mentioned above. Consolidating this pluralism, he believes, is necessary in order to avoid the 'reductionism' involved in looking 'for a single dominant institutional nexus' [55]. And yet by the end of the first section of chapter 2, the reader has learned: that capitalism preceded and largely generated industrialism [61]; that the monopoly of violence commanded by the modern state is connected with the extrusion of force from the labour process due to the changed 'nature of class domination' brought about by capitalism [62]; and that the 'insulation' of politics and economics which produces the modern sovereign form of state is one of the 'specific institutional features' [56] of capitalist societies.

Given that the four institutional clusters are supposed to enjoy some intellectual equivalence, the enormous role played by one in the others (which is not reciprocated in this account by any equivalent set of determinations running the other way) is remarkable. What is even more remarkable is that even where it supposedly meets its limits, the additional phenomena invoked by Giddens are still not ones to which he gives a definition or explanation in terms of the binding of space and time. The intake of extraneous concepts is rather accelerated. '[S]tates', he insists, in the most significant instance of this, 'derive their power from their sovereign capabilities' [72]. Now, few would doubt that modern sovereignty does indeed involve a particular binding of space and time. But such a claim could be made descriptively about any aspect of human existence. And the argument has still to be made as to why the binding of space and time – rather than the social characteristics of sovereignty which reconfigure space and time in this way – should provide the starting point for analysis.

Giddens does his best intermittently to reverse the stream of implications here: 'Behind these institutional clusterings', he reasserts at the conclusion of this section, 'lie the three sources of the dynamism of modernity distinguished earlier: time-space distantiation, disembedding, and reflexivity' [63]. But it is to no avail: the entire force of his own exposition implies that matters stand the other way about. At this crucial level of the institutional definition of modernity, the basic methodological shift required to ground 'globalisation' as an explanatory category (rather than just a flat, descriptive one) has simply not been carried out.

Now, it might be argued in Giddens' defence that the emergence of the four institutional clusters themselves depended on earlier historical transformations involving reconfigurations of space and time. But unless one is going (as his theory enjoins and the phrase 'sources of dynamism' certainly implies) to derive the institutional clusters of modernity causally from these, such a claim remains of indeterminate explanatory significance for the contemporary world. After all, in a similar way, Marx averred that 'thousands of centuries' of development were involved in the emergence of even the most primitive systems of commodity exchange – but he did not for that reason abandon the significance of the specifically capitalist form for explaining the modern world.

Thus, to revert to the metaphor employed by Ankie Hoogvelt, for all we know at this stage, globalisation as an historical process may well have 'lifted off'. And the read-out on Giddens' screen may even tell him that his own social theory has set off in pursuit. On the launch-pad itself, however, the intellectual engines of 'time-space distantiation' have not yet been started. We seem to have witnessed a special kind of theoretical malfunction – the phantom lift-off.

Definition by Trampoline

We should therefore watch very carefully as Giddens now works his way up to formulating what has become one of the most influential definitions of globalisation in the literature on the subject. The process occurs in four steps, which draw together some of the key elements of the discussion so far. First, he reminds us of the foundational quality of his argument, requiring as it does the replacement of traditional sociological categories by 'the problematic of time-space distantiation'. Second, he spells out the methodological implication of this shift, which is to refocus our attention on the *spatial* configuration of human agency, enabling us to analyse the social world specifically in terms of the interrelations of presence and absence, locality and distance involved in its reproduction. Next, the phrase 'time-space distantiation' is reinvoked. This time, however, its meaning has shifted. It has been narrowed down from a general intellectual problematic into something like a quantitative measure of the spatial and temporal distance across which social relations can be sustained in different historical worlds. 'In the modern era,' he tells us, 'the level of time-space distantiation is much higher than in any previous period.' The double consequence of this higher level is a geographical 'stretching' of social relations, together with the resultant proliferation of 'phantasmagoric spaces' – local sites of social reproduction which are increasingly interpenetrated with remote sources of causality. And this, finally, provides the bridge to the eventual definition: 'Globalisation can thus be defined as the intensification of worldwide social relations which link distant localities in such a way that local happenings are shaped by events occurring many miles away and vice versa' [64].

The movement of the argument here is so smoothly executed that it will take a minute to find the surface wrinkles which can lead us to the conceptual elisions taking place inside. The rhetorical flow of this sequence of propositions is clear enough. It *looks* like time-space distantiation is explaining globalisation – either in the sense that globalisation is a product of time-space distantiation (viewed as a tendential property of modernity), or in the sense that globalisation is quintessentially a spatial phenomenon, which the specialised categories of time-space distantiation (viewed as a problematic) uniquely enable us to analyse. And we can also see why this definition has proven so influential. For if either of these implicit claims could be made to stick, then the term 'globalisation' would indeed become more than just a descriptive geographical category. It would then reappear as the master category which uniquely captures both the expansive dynamic of modernity and the transformations in the very social texture of space itself. Time-space distantiation, wobbling back and forth between a theory and a problematic, therefore seems to provide the crucial link which grounds the concept of globalisation in a broader account of the social world.

The problem, however, is that each of the implicit claims referred to above rests on a prior assumption that spatio-temporal definitions of social phenomena are the key to explaining the historical character of modernity. And it is exactly this which neither Giddens nor anyone else has yet been able to establish. On the contrary, as we have already seen, in Giddens' own analysis spatio-temporal phenomena turn out again and again to be derivative of other institutional features of modernity which are not themselves defined in these terms. And because these other features – the *explanans* which should hold 'globalisation' firmly in place as an *explanandum* – are excluded from the eventual construction of the definition, the latter's steps must end up tracing a circular path.

First the reification of space which lurks within the concept of globalisation is read back into a reconstitution of the basic elements of social theory. There it seems to legitimate an intellectual inversion in which analysis of the social construction of space gives way to analysis of the spatial construction of societies. One might think that these two are not separable from each other. Yet – compounding the reification – the second step apparently proceeds as if they were, elaborating what it asserts to be an alternative set of analytical categories (locality, distance, presence, absence). Since what has prompted this spatialising of social theory is the peculiarly modern experience of time-space compression, we should not be surprised when step three identifies an historically unprecedented level of time-space distantiation as characteristic of modernity. Finally, from the resultant claim that 'modernity is inherently globalising', it is but a short step to the view that 'globalisation' is a master concept not just because it identifies an historical outcome in spatial terms, but because, being empty of any referent except a spatial one, it is the ideal carrier for both a substantive definition of modernity in spatio-temporal terms, and an abstract reformulation of theoretical categories in spatial terms. It thereby is made to appear both as the climax of a theory of modernity and as the bearer of a new intellectual paradigm.

What has really happened, however, is that an apparent grounding of globalisation in a broader social theory has in fact detached the concept from any deeper explanation than that contained in its own definition. And the idea of time-space distantiation plays a crucial role here, expanding the reach of spatial categories by colonising the deeper levels of substantive and abstract theory. It is this which finally closes the loop, and prevents the re-entry of non-spatio-temporal concepts which would otherwise re-transform the term 'globalisation' back into a purely descriptive one. By thus silencing in theory what has already proved impossible to exclude in practice, Giddens can make it appear as if 'globalisation' rests securely on an underlying social theory. In fact, however, that underlying social theory functions simply as an echo chamber for the concept, from which its own descriptive utterances return to it in the more sonorous form of explanatory propositions, and as if they derived from a separate and deeper source.

To put it another way, it is only by bouncing around on the trampoline of time-space distantiation that the concept of globalisation eventually gains sufficient intellectual altitude to leap over the logical barriers which would otherwise prevent this *explanandum* from occupying the logical space of an *explanans* in its own right.

However, the game is far from over. For Giddens has not yet finished unfurling his theory. His next steps involve him in a sequence of ethnomethodological, psychological and anthropological applications/ derivations of it. And the first of these now leads us conveniently away from the 'rear' of the problematic and round to the 'front', where we may next observe a quite spectacular collapse of substantive explanation.

Trouble Up Front

Here in chapter 3, almost for the first time, the theory of time-space distantiation is used to formulate and to answer questions about the basic characteristics of modern social life. The first of these questions is derived quite simply. As the level of time-space distantiation rises, more and more people are dependent upon networks of social relations which extend far beyond the local environments of individual human experience. Moreover, those social relations themselves have a disembedded, depersonalised quality – which is the precondition of their spatial extension in the first place. Symbolic tokens and expert systems are the great disembedding mechanisms of modernity – the abstract systems which effect 'the "lifting out" of social relations from local contexts of interaction and their restructuring across indefinite spans of time-space' [21]. In so doing, they generate a world of humanly created causes and consequences which differs from any pre-modern equivalent in two fundamental respects. First, because these abstract systems now govern and even constitute the basic conditions of life, participation in the dominant knowledge forms associated with them becomes compulsory:

> Individuals in pre-modern settings, in principle and in practice, could ignore the pronouncements of priests, sages and sorcerers and get on with the routines of daily activity. But this is not the case in the modern world, in respect of expert knowledge. [84]

And second, the subjective content of the confidence placed in such authority is also transformed:

> [It] is not just a matter . . . of generating a sense of security about an independently given universe of events. It is a matter of the calculation of benefit and risk in circumstances where expert knowledge does not just provide that calculus but actually *creates* . . . the universe of events, as a result of the continual reflexive implementation of that very knowledge. [84]

Thus, in a world governed by abstract systems, the routine generation of trust is both more vital and more problematic than ever before. The question therefore arises: how is this routine generation of trust accomplished? And Giddens' answer is that the fabric of modern life necessarily involves a particular recombination of co-presence and absence by which disembedded relations are 're-embedded' in local contexts of consciousness and action. Lay participation in abstract systems – such as banking, medicine, law or bureaucratically ordered government – requires a 'faceless commitment', a faith in the system itself which cannot be based either on direct personal experience of the whole or on a full technical understanding of the mechanisms and processes involved in its operation. Instead, it is sustained by the 'facework' involved in 'focused interactions' with 'system representatives' – bank employees, doctors, judges, state officials, and so on. These 'focused interactions' constitute the 'access points' which mediate the relation of the lay individual to the abstract system, and through which confidence in the system is maintained (if all goes well) by 'displays of manifest trustworthiness and integrity, coupled with an attitude of "business-as-usual", or unflappability' [85]. By these means, a system whose operation and extent lie beyond any lay understanding is able to reinsert itself into local contexts of meaningful action. Or as Giddens puts it: 'Reembedding refers to processes by means of which faceless commitments are sustained or transformed by facework' [88].

Giddens in fact adds two further elements of an explanation for why lay trust is routinely granted to abstract systems: a process of socialisation normalises acceptance of their role in mundane activities; and the practical impossibility of conducting daily life without interacting with them imposes a pragmatic imperative of tacit reliance. However, most of Giddens' interest remains focused on the role of 'access points' – presumably because it is in that part of his analysis that spatial categories play the most significant role. Here at last, Giddens has foregrounded the complex texture of social space under conditions of time-space distantiation. We can now therefore begin to assess the explanatory benefit of the overall shift of theoretical problematic which he has been advocating. What then may we say that it enables us to understand?

And this is where the collapse begins. For posing such a question cannot help but make one consider the range of things about social structures which one would indeed want explained. And yet what strikes one immediately in this context is the kind of phenomena which in Giddens' new perspective actually cease to be objects of analysis and explanation at all. For although abstract systems of vast extent loom very large in this discussion, the causal properties of these systems, rooted in the social form of the relationships which compose them, drop more or less out of sight. And this is because when they are viewed through the lens of time-space distantiation, their most significant attribute becomes instead their shared 'disembeddedness' from local contexts which makes possible their indefinite spatial extension. Such a focus, however, cannot help but evacuate these systems of their differentiated social content. Flattened out in this way, the world market, the state, law, medicine, science – even the travel industry – take on the same fundamental character: so many disembodied knowledge-structures which increasingly permeate the routine activities of everyday life even while they expand (both geographically and technically) further and further beyond the horizon of individual consciousness. This perhaps explains why the only significant question they raise should be that of how trust in such uncomprehended knowledge-structures is locally generated and maintained – and in turn why Giddens' answer to this question must take a mainly descriptive, ethnomethodological form. For to elucidate the objective causal properties of the systems themselves – that is, to explain how and why they operate to distribute wealth and knowledge and power in particular ways – it would be necessary to go beyond an analysis of their spatio-temporal articulation. And since this would carry him outside the problematic of time-space distantiation, it is perhaps understandable that Giddens does not attempt it. The consequence, however, is that his own account is restricted to a series of descriptive banalities, dressed up in a pseudo-technical language – access points, faceless commitments, facework, focused interactions, system representatives, etc. – by an author who earlier prefaced the construction of his argument with the warning that 'it is not sufficient merely to invent new terms' [3]. Well then: do we really need 'a fresh characterisation . . . of the nature of modernity' [4] in order to see that we are routinely involved in big systems which we do not generally understand; that this involvement is mediated by bureaucratic organisations in which the impersonal rules of the system are re-embodied in the behavioural codes of the employees; and that our confidence in the systems can be undermined by incompetent or unprofessional behaviour? It is not that one finds anything here to disagree with. But one cannot help being struck by what a drastic reduction of the explanatory claims of social theory has occurred. And the reason is not far to seek. If time-space distantiation is taken seriously as an alternative problematic, the price that is paid is effectively the externalising of the social dynamics of the systems themselves.

The Argument Regroups

Still, if the theory of time-space distantiation appears to lack ambition in the opening sections of chapter 3 [79–88], this is more than compensated for in the next section, where the scope of its claims is suddenly and dramatically extended – and that in a quite unexpected direction. We noted in the Introduction to this chapter, when setting out the four steps of the overall argument, that a curious phenomenon occurs, in which step three of the argument (application) suddenly reaches back into step two (formulation) in order to re-inject in a new form the explanatory human content whose progressive evacuation from the structures of social life has been such a marked and disabling feature of the theory so far. The most striking of these retrospective adjustments is now about to happen.

For at this point, Giddens temporarily turns his back on the 'institutional analysis of modernity' [1] which forms the main object of his argument, and focuses instead on 'aspects of trust and processes of personality development which seem to apply in all cultures, pre-modern and modern' [92]. The purpose of this detour, it later transpires, is nothing less than an attempt to reground the problematic of time-space distantiation in the findings of psychoanalytic theory. His starting point is the phenomenon of 'ontological security . . . the confidence that most human beings have in the continuity of their self-identity and in the constancy of the surrounding social and material environments of action' [92]. Without this confidence, individuals become incapable of relating to others and are consumed by various forms of 'existential anxiety'. Now, at a purely cognitive level, as 'philosophers have shown us' [92], the beliefs which make for ontological security – beliefs in the continuity of the self and the reliable existence of external reality – cannot be verified. So why, asks Giddens, 'is everyone not always in a state of high ontological insecurity . . .?' [94].

This question is slightly odd, since he has already pointed out that ontological security 'is an emotional, rather than a cognitive, phenomenon' [92], and sceptical philosophers 'are not, we may suppose, ontologically insecure' [93]. But it provides the bridge to the argument he wishes to make. For he answers it in psychological terms: '"Normal" individuals, I want to argue, receive a basic "dosage" of trust in early life that deadens or blunts these existential susceptibilities' [94]. Specifically, maternal love provides both a primal experience of the reliability of the external world and a framework of mutual expectations between mother and infant; meeting the latter promotes 'an inner sense of trustworthiness, which provides a basis of a stable self-identity subsequently' [94].

Once again, this psychological claim about the nature of infantile development may well be true. What takes the breath away, however, is the astonishing intellectual compression of the inferences which Giddens now attempts to draw out of it. 'A faith in the caretaker's love is the essence of that leap to commitment which basic trust – and all forms of trust thereafter – presumes' [95]. *All* forms of trust? Since it is Giddens himself who has earlier proposed a sociological use of the term (trust) in relation to abstract systems, the trap that he falls into at this point is entirely of his own making. For although there do exist forms of neurosis which disable this latter form of trust, this is hardly sufficient to prove the general claim he wants to make about the continuity of psychological and sociological forms of trust.[51] After all, psychopaths, who presumably did not receive their 'basic "dosage" of trust in early life', are not known for their inability to trust abstract systems. On the contrary, more often they appear to thrive in them, manipulating the confidence of others which is based on exactly that conflation of functional competence (ethnomethodological as well as bureaucratic) with psychological normalcy which is implied in Giddens' argument here. If it really were true that 'all forms of trust' presume the basic dosage, then catching psychopaths would be hugely simplified. In fact, it might even be unnecessary since their functional incompetence would be so pronounced that no-one would be taken in by them in the first place.

However, an unexpected climax to the argument now approaches. Having slipped (in his opening question) between the philosophical and psychological meanings of uncertainty, and having then conflated (in his answer) the psychological and sociological referents of the term 'trust', Giddens proceeds to what must be the most daring compression of all. Central to the originary exercises in infantile identity-formation, he observes, is a crucial spatio-temporal element. The alternating presence and absence of the mother both creates the 'space' in which an independent sense of self can crystallise and nurtures the child's ability to believe in the mother's return even while she is still absent. In this way, the infant is in fact led to develop an emotional and cognitive faculty – trust – whose essence is that it 'brackets distance in time and space' [97] and thereby fends off all manner of existential anxieties which might otherwise supervene. Thus a side-effect of the spatial character of our early development of ontological security is that we all receive as babies a basic training in the psychosocial dynamics of globalisation. If this interpretation of Giddens' argument appears ridiculous, it should be set alongside the conclusion which he himself draws: 'Here, at the heart of the psychological development of trust, we rediscover the problematic of time-space distantiation' [97].

Now, exactly what weight is this revelatory announcement supposed to carry? Some of the difficulties of Giddens' overall argument so far could perhaps be mitigated if we simply excised the last few steps and allowed the problematic of time-space distantiation to resume a more consistently sociological provenance. The problem, however, is that Giddens himself has other plans. For him the psychological derivation of the concept of ontological security was not a detour at all. It was a journey to the epicentre of the entire argument, from which he now returns with implications of a very far-reaching kind. In the next section, the changing conditions making for ontological security become the axis about which an extended contrast between premodern and modern societies is made to turn (the most detailed contrast of modernity with premodernity in the whole book). And after the implications of this have been worked back into an analysis of the constitution of the modern, globalised self in chapter 4, it undergoes a further expansion, becoming the basis for a comprehensive reimagining of the possibilities and forms of political action in the contemporary world.

Far from ignoring it, therefore, we must now trace its influence in the remainder of his argument: for the changing anthropological conditions of ontological security are now also being used to provide the alternative filling for his social theory, apparently sealing off at the same time the gaps at the 'rear' through which more traditional concepts had earlier reinserted themselves. And because it is indeed the spatio-temporal transformations in the conditions of ontological security which from now on form the main theme, we for our part are forced to take seriously a possibility which in all the preceding criticisms we have not even paused properly to consider, let alone do justice to: the possibility that viewed in this new light – and fully in line with the very title of the book – these (spatio-temporal) *consequences* of modernity, by transforming the conditions of ontological security, might actually have become over time of greater importance than the 'original' causal dynamics which generated them, and that they therefore *legitimately* displace the latter in the analysis of the contemporary world.

If this argument could be made to stick, its knock-on effects would be enormous. Our entire critique of Giddens' position would start to unravel: our complaint that his intellectual categories do not illuminate the inner causal mechanisms of different abstract systems would prove only that we had spectacularly missed the point of his analysis; on the other hand, his advocacy of a spatio-temporal problematic for social theory would be decisively vindicated; and globalisation theory would have found in 'time-space distantiation' that theoretical underpinning which we have up to now insisted it could not logically possess. At the same time, however, if the movement of the argument has unexpectedly forced us onto the back foot at this point, it has also quite dramatically raised the stakes on the other side. A hypothetical possibility now has to be substantiated. In order for the argument to stick, it must be shown that changes in the spatio-temporal conditions of ontological security are the most causally significant feature of 'high modernity'.

What, then, is the essence of the shift in the conditions of ontological security or trust which distinguishes the modern from the premodern world? In answering this question, Giddens for the first time constructs his wider argument in unambiguously spatio-temporal terms: the shift concerns the institutional means by which these types of society differently organise themselves in space and time, their contrasted 'modes of organising 'reliable' interactions across time-space' [101]. Of these, he singles out four as characteristic of the premodern world.

First, kinship systems can bracket time and space, by providing a principle of mutual obligation among family members which is generally recognised irrespective of whether particular individuals are emotionally close to, or even personally acquainted with, each other. Second, in premodern times, 'local community' provided a context for the generating of trust relations because its 'space' was more or less socially self-contained, and was not yet saturated with 'distanciated time-space relations' extending beyond local control. (It had not yet become 'phantasmagoric'.) A stable sense of 'place' could therefore be reproduced via 'clusters of interweaving social relations, the low spatial span of which provides for their solidity in time' [101–3]. A third pre-modern support of trust relations is provided by religious cosmology, which 'contributes to the bracketing of time-space' [104] by imparting a reliability to social and natural events through interpreting them as meaningful expressions of a supernatural order. Indeed, Giddens, following Freud, sees religious cosmologies as a projection onto external reality of the infantile experience of parental care relations. Finally, there is the role of 'tradition' – that mode of choreographing social practices in space and time which connects past, present and future as mutually reinforcing parts of a reliable temporal whole. Bracketed in this way, the passage of time is transformed from a journey into the unknown, into a self-confirming cycle of dependable events across which trust relations can (therefore) be extended, and from which support for ontological security can be derived.

Giddens' purpose here is of course not to imply that premodern societies were necessarily more comfortable than modern ones; they had their own 'risk profile' associated with natural hazards, endemic localised violence and the fear of personal damnation. His point is rather that each of these ways of organising time-space as a medium of those trust relations through which social orders are reproduced has now been fatally eroded by the rise of modern social forms. Kinship has been largely displaced by abstract systems, locality by phantasmagoric space, religious cosmology by secular science, and tradition by 'the reflexivity of modern social life' [109]. And correspondingly, a new and different 'risk profile' now stalks the psycho-sociological horizon, dominated by the instability and side-effects of abstract systems, the heightened destructiveness of state-centralised, industrialised warfare and the intrinsic meaninglessness of the human and natural worlds unavoidably propounded by the discourse of modern science.

On the basis of this contrast, we can now formulate more explicitly than before exactly what the problematic of time-space distantiation comprises. Its fundamental premise is not simply the observation that different societies organise themselves differently in space and time, and may fruitfully be studied in this aspect. After all, the comparative analysis of territorialities and temporalities across a range of human cultures has long formed a part of the stock in trade of anthropological and other research, without being advanced as the core problematic for social theory as a whole. What brings it centre-stage in Giddens' work is an anterior theoretical claim: that relations of trust – without which neither the ontological security of the individual nor the reproduction of social orders can be sustained – are *fundamentally constituted through the bracketing of space and time.* And for this reason, to analyse the institutional forms in which this bracketing is accomplished in any given case is to dissect *the very substance of society itself.*[52]

For time-space distantiation, it now becomes clear, does not become important only when its 'level' is high, stretching the web of social relations into worldwide systems. The very fact of the existence of human beings as discrete centres of consciousness, separate both from other humans and from nature, unable therefore to have continuous certainty about the inner workings and future behaviour of either – this fact entails that there will *always* be a gap to be bridged through the bracketing of space and time which enables trust, even in the most localised of face-to-face communities. Nothing less could explain how Giddens can meaningfully 'rediscover the problematic of time-space distantiation' even in the most biologically and psychologically intimate of all human relations, that of an infant to its mother. For it follows that the primordial differentiation of the human individual itself can only occur through the training in the bracketing of space and time. Time-space distantiation begins at the moment we emerge from the womb.

Here then finally we are given a reason, grounded in a general social theory, for that shift of problematic which Giddens has been advocating from the start of the book, but which up to now has lacked any firm foundation. Leaving aside any methodological misgivings about the conflation of sociological with psychological determinations, what can we say about the explanatory power of the overall theory, now that its different components have all finally snapped into place? In chapters 4 and 5 Giddens provides some key materials for answering this question. For although he begins with an analysis of 'the transformation of intimacy', he soon returns to the macrosociological level to elaborate the globalised risk profile of modernity, and to reinterpret in that light the nature and possibilities of political action.

Hide and Seek with Space and Time

Chapter 4 therefore now becomes critical in substantiating the claims of time-space distantiation. And the one charge which cannot be levelled at Giddens at this point is that he shirks the enormity of the challenge by scaling down the ambition of those claims. 'Any attempt to capture the experience of modernity', he insists, two-thirds of the way through the chapter, 'must begin from [a] view . . . which derives ultimately from the dialectics of space and time, as expressed in the time-space constitution of modern institutions' [139]. Moreover, these 'dialectics of space and time' are now repeatedly invoked directly in terms of their consequences for 'ontological security' within an implied spatial model of causal implications: in the three main parts of this chapter, the globalisation of social relations is claimed explicitly to be fundamental to (successively) the changing nature of the human self, the overarching risk profile of modernity and the unique historical form of modern human agency.

It might therefore awaken a natural scepticism in the reader to be told that the major problem with this chapter lies in its apparent failure even to argue for these claims, let alone to substantiate them. Yet this is exactly what we shall now discover, as we work our way through it, page by page.

Every so often, we shall see Giddens popping up to make a bold declaration of the kind just quoted. But before the reader can catch him and hold him to his word, he ducks down again behind a thicket of descriptive elaboration. And by the time we have worked our way through the thicket, we find he has already moved on, only to pop up again at a different point in the field, with a new and equally tantalising declaration. The chapter thereby resolves into a gigantic game of hide and seek, played out across the wide terrain of contemporary social theory. In the version of the game which we are about to play, however, there is a crucial difference to the rules. And it is not always clear that Giddens has grasped it. Ducking and weaving is permitted, up to a point; but in the end, if he cannot be caught and pinned down, his argument collapses, and it is he (and not the baffled reader) who loses the game.

The reason for this change in the rules is very simple. Giddens can potentially save globalisation theory and neutralise nearly all the major criticisms we have made of the work so far. All he must do to achieve this is to substantiate what we have now discovered to be the central claim of the work as a whole: namely, that changes in the spatio-temporal conditions of ontological security are the most causally significant feature of modernity. If he fails to achieve this, however, then all those previous criticisms will automatically resume their full destructive force – supplemented by whatever further liabilities he may have incurred in the meantime.

From the very start of chapter 4, Giddens' language suggests that he has every intention of providing this substantiation. He wastes no time in issuing his first bold declaration: '[T]here is a direct (though dialectical) connection between the globalising tendencies of modernity and what I shall call the *transformation of intimacy* in contexts of day-to-day life' [114]. From this point onwards, the argument of the chapter unfolds in three stages. The first stage [pp. 114–24] works down from the spread of abstract systems at the macrosociological level to the changed conditions of trust which they entail at the level of the individual. The second [pp. 124–37] repeats the exercise with respect to the impact of the risk profile of modernity on conditions of ontological security. Finally, the third stage [pp. 137–49] reasserts the 'dialectical' nature of the analysis by revisioning each of these as a site of active human agency. Thus, as this unpacking implies, the expansive scope of Giddens' opening declaration is not unintended: the entire theory is surely about to be cashed in.

Thicket #1: The Transformation of Intimacy

The first stage of the argument is set up as follows. In the routines of day-to-day life, abstract systems must be recognised to provide a vastly enhanced security of human activities across time-space. And in our practice, we do so recognise them. Turning taps, sending letters, flying in aeroplanes, saving money – all these actions imply a pragmatic trust in the abstract systems on which modern life depends. However, there are some things which they cannot provide. In contrast to their pre-modern antecedents, the world-religions (which bound space and time in ways that were explicitly meaningful and personalised), trust in abstract systems is not psychologically rewarding. Indeed, in a nuance which stands in some tension with his earlier statements (but which is nonetheless necessary if the argument is to develop at this point), Giddens now tells us that '[n]on-personalised trust . . . is discrepant from basic trust' [120], and that this discontinuity underlies the significance of access points since the latter 'provide the link between personal and system trust' [115].

How, then, does the nomenclature of trust enable us to reconceptualise the rise of modernity with respect to the interrelation of individual and community? Giddens begins by rejecting three '[e]stablished sociological accounts' [115]: the conservative lament at the collapse of communal values and the turning inward of individuals to refocus on selfish interests; the Habermasian picture of a life-world increasingly invaded and colonised by the instrumentally rational determinations of depersonalised social forms and institutions; and the counter-claim made by some urban sociologists that 'community' in the traditional sense re-establishes itself in the apparently inhospitable settings of modern city life. All these positions, says Giddens, share a common flaw: an undifferentiated conception of 'community', deriving ultimately from an uncritical acceptance of Ferdinand Tönnies classical contrast of *Gemeinschaft* and *Gesellschaft*. And it is this essentialised notion of community which can be broken down by distinguishing the contrasting combinations of 'trust mechanisms' which compose and recompose it in different historical circumstances.

At the heart of 'traditional' forms of community, Giddens identifies four such mechanisms: 'communal relations per se' [117] (based on enclosed local interdependence), kinship relations, ties of friendship and sexual relations. By contrast, in the contemporary world the first two of these have 'indeed largely been destroyed' [117] by the rise of abstract systems which both transcend the spatial limits of locality and 'explicitly overcome dependency upon personal ties' [119]. The other two, however, far from being holed up in some shrinking institutional redoubt called the private/personal sphere, have themselves been transformed in ways that cannot be registered using crude dichotomies such as public/private, impersonal/personal, or *Gesellschaft/Gemeinschaft*. A better understanding of the overall shift – part dissolution, part transformation – will be provided by observing the linkage between the 'globalising tendencies' and novel subjectivities of modernity.

In premodern societies, friendship was not just a contingent association of individuals. It was a directly communal institution. Sanctioned by publicly recognised codes of 'honour', it provided a mechanism (comparable to bonds of kinship and locality) by which personalised trust could be parlayed into 'social relations of a distanced sort, which stretch into "enemy territories"' [119]. By contrast, in modernity, where time-space distantiation is articulated via depersonalised, abstract systems, the nature and role of friendship are correspondingly transformed. It *appears* to be reconstituted as a 'purely personal' association: 'honour' is replaced by 'loyalty', publicly significant 'sincerity' by privately fostered 'authenticity', and so on. Yet this new 'purely personal' quality is not to be understood as somehow external to the world of abstract systems. For the latter provide not only the socio-historical condition of this new intersubjective form, but also a vehicle for its extension over much greater distances (via telecommunications) and even (in the shape of popularised psycho-analytic expertise) the very language of its private discursive formulation by the agents themselves.

What applies to friendship in general applies *a fortiori* to the yet more intimate sphere of sexual relations: unsupported by its interpolation into public institutions (through arranged marriages), personalised trust must instead be 'worked upon' in a 'mutual process of disclosure', yielding the historically novel social form of the 'relationship' as a 'project'. Indeed, because this 'disclosure' is at the same time a 'self-discovery', it exemplifies nothing less than a reaching into the sphere of the intimate by 'the reflexivity of modernity' itself [122]. Similar points, however, apply also to other features of supposedly personal life: 'It has long been the case, for example, that Western diets reflect global economic interchanges' [120]; and the spiritual preferences of Western consumers of religion are now serviced by a truly global menu.

All this, says Giddens, 'is not simply a diminishment of personal life in favour of impersonally organised systems – it is a genuine transformation of the nature of the personal itself' [120]. There can thus be no retreat from the globalised abstract systems into a protected personal sphere, for the latter has no separate existence.

Well, there is the first thicket. Before we go inside, and without wishing to tax the patience of the reader with all too familiar lines of argument, there is something which can already be said about it, even from this distance. Despite the mantle of novelty which Giddens tries to draw round the discussion – 'Friendship has rarely been studied by sociologists' [118] – the actual object of the analysis here is, once again, one of the most prominent themes of classical social theory: namely, the historicity of the individual as a social form. Marx, Weber, Durkheim – they all meditated at some length on the particular reconfiguration of inner and outer worlds within which this new and paradoxical form of human subject was constituted. Not for them – not for *any* of them – those essentialised, dehistoricised categories of community and selfhood which serve as the springboard for this portion of Giddens' 'fresh characterisation of modernity'. In fact, the superficial similarities of Giddens' alternative to Marx's account are so striking that it would be altogether churlish to deny the original some voice in the proceedings at this point.

For it was of course Marx who argued that in modernity 'individuals are now ruled by *abstractions*'[53] – forms of interrelation which are 'abstracted' from the personal particularities of those individuals; and, moreover, that in a society organised via these abstractions – rather than via 'relations of personal dependence' – the nature of selfhood is itself transformed. The non-differentiation of personal and social identity which Giddens registers in his discussion of premodern friendship conforms to Marx's observation that in societies based on 'relations of personal dependence', people 'enter into connection with one another only as individuals imprisoned within a certain definition'.[54] By contrast, says Marx, the members of modern society 'have become abstract individuals, who are, however, by this very fact put in a position to enter into relation with one another *as individuals*'.[55] 'Here,' adds Derek Sayer, in a perceptive discussion of these points, 'personal relations appear – for the first time – *as* "purely" personal, as distinct from social. . . . The individual is now conceivable, as a subject, independently of social contexts.'[56] Needless to say, the last thing this entailed for Marx was the intellectual windmill which Giddens spends his pages tilting at: namely, that the emergent monadic quality of 'the individual' as subject warranted its analytical counterposition to 'the social'. On the contrary, he insisted that 'the epoch which produces this standpoint, that of the isolated individual, is precisely the epoch of the hitherto most developed . . . relations.'[57]

However, we should not be distracted by these points from the main issue. Giddens is supposed to be demonstrating that changes in the spatio-temporal conditions of ontological security are the most causally significant feature of high modernity. And his first step has been to assert the connection between globalisation and the transformation of intimacy. How far, then, does this contribute to such a demonstration? The answer must hinge on the nature of the connection he is able to establish. If, as the discussion of community seems at first to imply, it is the demise of spatial enclosure which causes (even 'dialectically') the transformation of intimacy, then this would mark a large step indeed. A closer inspection of the argument, however, reveals that matters do not quite stand that way.

There is a loose thread which needs weaving back in if the fabric of such an argument is not to come apart. In Giddens' account, spatial enclosure is not the only support of traditional community which has been dissolved by 'the consequences of modernity'. There is a second: kinship relations. Why has this role of kinship relations dissolved? Because abstract systems 'explicitly overcome dependency on personal ties' [119]. Is it their globalising spatial extent which enables them to overcome this dependency? No. Again on Giddens' account, it is rather their depersonalised character (resting on symbolic tokens and expertise) which allows for their indefinite socio-spatial extension. But if that is the case, if there are other causes operating in the destruction of kinship as a principle of social organisation, then why should we hold that it is the specifically spatial ('globalising') tendencies of modernity which lie at the root of the transformation of intimacy?

Now, it might be thought that this is hardly a problem: Giddens has explicitly embraced a causal pluralism. How therefore can acceptance of additional causes damage his central argument? The answer is that even Giddens' pluralism is, intellectually speaking, a 'bounded entity' – as it would have to be to avoid complete analytic indeterminacy. It is important, therefore, that any additional causes he invokes should at least fall within the intellectual borders of his argument. And the particular causes involved here are ones which he himself has expelled from that argument at an earlier point.

To appreciate the truly strategic nature of the problem here, we must go back to the first chapter, where Giddens lays out the definitional groundwork of his explanatory categories, and we must look in particular at his discussion of 'disembedding'. This term derives from the work of the economic anthropologist Karl Polanyi, who used it to describe the institutional differentiation of market relationships into a self-regulating sphere of 'the economy'. In pre-capitalist societies, Polanyi argued, markets were by contrast 'embedded in social relations',[58] and thereby subordinated to 'non-economic' constraints of various kinds. In its original meaning, therefore, 'disembedding' referred to one aspect of that wider institutional 'differentiation of spheres' which so many social theorists have seen as characteristic of the emergence of modern societies.

This, however, is not what Giddens means by the term:

> By disembedding I mean the 'lifting out' of social relations from local contexts of interaction and their restructuring across indefinite spans of time-space. [21]

Moreover, Giddens makes it clear that this spatio-temporal definition of 'disembedding' is offered as a *replacement* for those 'concepts of "differentiation"' by which '[s]ociologists have often discussed the transition from the traditional to the modern world', on the grounds that, among other problems, the latter do 'not satisfactorily address the issue of time-space distantiation' [21]. Thus, in Giddens' hands, 'disembedding' becomes a term to be deployed in explanatory opposition to its original (unacknowledged) meaning.[59]

This is the kind of intellectual procedure which has made Giddens so famously difficult to pin down. For once, however, the implication is crystal clear: Giddens has explicitly made the success of his overall argument dependent on the ability of 'disembedding' (redefined in spatio-temporal terms) fully to displace 'differentiation' (conventionally understood) as a basis for explaining the emergence and character of modern social forms. And indeed, from the point of view of globalisation theory, this is a necessary step: anything less would concede an ontologically derivative status to spatial and temporal phenomena, and would thereby undermine the claim of time-space distantiation to constitute an alternative problematic for social theory.

Yet it is this same foundational move which now returns to haunt the argument in this opening stage of chapter 4. As we have seen, Giddens states that the decline of kinship as an organisational principle rests upon the capacity of abstract systems to 'explicitly overcome dependency on personal ties'. But unless that capacity can be shown itself to derive from the spatio-temporal attributes of abstract systems, such a claim simply re-opens the case for an antecedent process of institutional differentiation as the most significant feature of the rise of modern social forms. Giddens himself seems not to notice this problem. Not only does he make no attempt at a spatio-temporal regrounding of his observations on kinship; on the contrary, he extends the problem by applying the same observations to friendship and sexuality. It is, after all, now Giddens himself who defines 'the transformation of intimacy' as an historical process by which personal ties, which were once publicly interpolated with social relations (via honorific friendship and arranged marriage), lose this wider role, becoming reconstituted in new and apparently separate spheres of action and meaning. It would be hard to imagine a more faithful reproduction of the intellectual schema of 'differentiation' by which '[s]ociologists have often discussed the transition from the traditional to the modern world'. But this is not a fidelity which Giddens' argument at this point can afford: for the more he relies on this schema, the more he becomes subject to his own earlier criticism of it. And it is not at all clear how his definitional reformulation of it could be said to more 'satisfactorily address the issue of time-space distantiation'.

What certainly should be clear by now is the following. There may indeed be direct connections between 'the transformation of intimacy' and 'the globalising tendencies of modernity'. Those direct connections, however, are not the most significant ones for explaining either of these phenomena, and they therefore cannot begin to bear the weight which the ambitions of this chapter place upon them. Although Giddens claims that we 'must begin from [a] view . . . which derives ultimately from the dialectics of space and time', the evidence of his own practice stands against any such premise. When push comes to shove, his own 'attempt to capture the experience of modernity' tacitly reverts to the previously discarded 'differentiation of spheres' which – it now turns out – ultimately stands behind both the personal and the spatial transformations he is trying to connect and explain. All of which, intellectually speaking, returns us to the state of play as it was left by the classical social theorists themselves.

Well, these observations do not finally settle the matter. Giddens may still be right in his central claim. But they do entail, against initial appearances, that the argument so far has still not begun to substantiate that claim. However, there is no point in delaying any longer inside this thicket. Giddens himself has not tarried to engage us on these points. Before we have time to finish our cleaning-up operation here, he has already popped up again elsewhere to issue his next bold declaration. It starts with a headline emphasis on the 'globalisation of risk' [124]. And the stakes therefore rise once again as we head off towards the second thicket.

Thicket #2: Risk and Ontological Security

There seem to be two dimensions to this next stage. On the one hand, the movement of the description retraces the top-down path of the first stage, moving this time not from abstract systems to interpersonal relations, but rather from the global risk profile of modernity down to its impact on the ontological security of individuals. This adds a second thread to the interweaving of the global and the personal – or as Giddens puts it, the 'extensional' and the 'intensional' [123]. At the same time, however, these pages also extend Giddens' alternative image of the fabric of modern social life – the image offered as a substitute for those visions based on the false dichotomy of *Gemeinschaft* and *Gesellschaft*. For if the latter were mistaken in their account of the relations between these two, they were nonetheless right about one thing: the modern world has indeed taken on a 'menacing appearance' which is full of significance for the life-world of individuals. And it is this 'menacing appearance' and its consequences which he now proposes to reinterpret via the categories of risk and ontological security.

Clearly, risk is going to be an important category in this discussion. And one therefore has a natural impulse to refer back at this point to the earlier discussion in chapter 1 for a definition. Alas, the reader should be warned against any such procedure: it will only breed confusion. For what does Giddens do in that earlier discussion [30ff.]? He lifts an apparently clear definition from the work of Luhmann, enters some caveats which supposedly open up a real conceptual difference, and then starts issuing categorical statements about risk which, in the absence of an actual redefinition, cannot now be referred back to any clear concept for purposes either of falsification or even comprehension. For this reason, the only sure guide we can have to what Giddens really means by risk is by practical inference from the descriptive content of the risk profile of modernity which he now sets out. We must enter the thicket.

The overall shape of this profile is traced by the interacting conjunction of two types of factors: those relating to the *objective scope* and character of the contingencies generated by modern societies; and those deriving from the *subjective form* in which those contingencies are experienced by the populations involved. So far as the first type of factors is concerned, Giddens lists four. There is the apocalyptic nature (or as he also puts it, 'global intensity' [125]) of certain socially produced contingencies – the possibility, for example, of 'nuclear war, ecological calamity, uncontainable population explosion, the collapse of global economic exchange' [125], and so on. Each of these 'transcends all social and economic differentials' [125]. Second, there is that quality of modern contingency which derives from the global spatial extension of abstract systems – namely, the objective loss of local control even when the system is functioning normally (let alone at points of breakdown). This dimension of risk rises with the expanding governance of more and more aspects of everyday life via globalising abstract systems. Next, the unintended ecological consequences of industrialisation add a third, distinctively modern, raft of contingencies rooted in '*socialised nature*: the infusion of human knowledge into the material environment' [124]. And finally, there is the uniquely consequential role played in modernity by 'institutionalised risk environments', in which contingency (in the form of guessing games between the actors about each other's calculations) refers no longer just to outcomes, but rather enters directly into and intensifies the recursive character of social behaviour itself. Situations governed in this way range from gambling and sports, through the behaviour of markets, and all the way to the nuclear arms race.

Meanwhile, the modern subjective experience of risk is characterised by three closely related features: first, the premodern assumption that risk of any kind could be assuaged by religious or magical techniques has largely passed away; second, this '*awareness of risk* as *risk*' [125] is widely distributed among the lay population, where, third, it is compounded by a sense of '*the limitations of expertise*' (in the sense both of the contingent incompleteness of understanding *and* of the inability in principle of reflexive knowledge to embrace in advance the unintended consequences of its own application).

Now, given Giddens' earlier discussion of the premodern 'environment of risk' which included 'threats and dangers emanating from *nature*' [see the table on p. 102], we cannot say that he defines risk in general as socially generated contingency. Such a definition would, however, apply very well to his description of the specifically modern risk environment (a point which, incidentally, carries him most of the way back into alignment with Luhmann's original definition). We may therefore summarise this passage as follows: by comparison with the premodern, the modern risk profile is dominated by forms of socially generated contingency which are more apocalyptic, more distantiated, more enmired in the consequences of socialised nature and the dilemmas of calculative rationality – and self-consciously so, in a culturally disenchanted and reflexively open-ended way.

The important question then becomes: what is the impact of all this on the ontological security of individuals, lately advanced as the centre of gravity of social reproduction? The answer seems to lie with the peculiar combination here of intensity, impersonality and intractability. Since it is altogether too traumatic to be thinking continuously of the consequences of nuclear war (though the apocalyptic scale of the threat certainly merits nothing less), a thin but impermeable layer of fatalism must be allowed to re-form over the surface of this contingency – 'a vague and generalised trust in distant events over which one has no control' [133]. This is a process assisted by the 'heavily counterfactual character of the most consequential risks' [134]: low probability puzzles the will by rendering insoluble the calculus of political engagement. Risk of this kind has paradoxical 'narcotising effects' [134]. And yet all this

> surely exacts a price on the level of the unconscious, since it essentially presumes the repression of anxiety. The sense of dread which is the antithesis of basic trust is likely to infuse unconscious sentiments about the uncertainties faced by humanity as whole. [133]

Given what we now know of the centrality of trust to the general theory of time-space distantiation, this should surely be read as a very serious observation indeed, one which must be replete with all manner of causal implications. Rather than draw these out, however, Giddens concludes this second stage of his exposition with a description of four 'adaptive reactions to the risk profile of modernity' [134]. Briefly, 'pragmatic acceptance . . . sustained optimism . . . cynical pessimism . . . [and] radical engagement' comprise a spectrum of subjective orientations through which individuals seek to cope with the 'menacing appearance' of modernity. It is significant to note that of these four, only the last finds a practical outlet (however partial) for the anxieties of modernity which are otherwise counterproductively repressed. And 'the social movement' which becomes 'the prime vehicle' of 'radical engagement' [137] provides thereby the point of reunification for psychological authenticity and social activism under conditions of modernity.

The chapter is building to its climax, in which a summative 'Phenomenology of Modernity' is about to be presented. Before the wave of accumulated analysis finally breaks over our heads, however, let us remind ourselves one last time exactly what is supposed to be being demonstrated here.

We saw in earlier sections that Giddens' claim to present 'a fresh characterisation of modernity' was repeatedly vitiated by reliance (acknowledged or otherwise) on the ideas of classical writers which he had supposedly discarded. We also saw that the theory of time-space distantiation could not explain – indeed, rested on an abstraction from – the differentiated social content of the various social structures of modernity. The prospects did not look good. What gave his argument a new lease of life was the sudden rise to prominence within it of a theme which, though present from the start, was now revealed to be its actual, central support: the theme of ontological security. And this was a development which, we acknowledged, had the capacity to pull off a retrospective rescue of the argument so far, by transforming our understanding of its terms.

Specifically, if, as indeed the title of the work implied, it was the *consequences* of modernity for ontological security which now turned out to be of greatest significance for understanding the contemporary world, then there would be no contradiction between drawing selectively on classical accounts of modernity while arguing nonetheless that they needed to be systematically transcended. (Marx might actually have understood a great deal about the inner workings of capitalism without, however, correctly grasping which of its unintended consequences would turn out to be most significant for the world which, at the time that he wrote, it was just beginning to transform.) And if, further, these consequences derived specifically from the shared spatio-temporal properties of abstract systems, then the differentiated social content of the latter, while not by any means unimportant, could safely be left for other theories to specify. Finally, if both the above claims were shown to be validated by the experience of 'high modernity', then not only would the term 'globalisation' be able to carry the theoretical weight we denied it; but also, the problematic of time-space distantiation would gain real credibility: for it would have provided the alternative categories by which the most significant aspects of the overall process could best be grasped.

If, if, if. The recurrent conditional reminds us that the role assigned to the theme of ontological security itself entailed some basic assumptions which now had to be substantiated if the entire argument were not once again to collapse. And these assumptions all pointed to a single, simple requirement: it must be shown, we said, that changes in the spatio-temporal conditions of ontological security are the most causally significant feature of 'high modernity'.

In this respect, chapter 4 got off to a poor start. In a further eruption of analytical havoc in the rear, the original meaning of 'disembedding' burst through the defensive wall of redefinition with which Giddens had earlier sought to exclude it, displacing within his own account the spatio-temporal causes of the transformation of intimacy and community. As for the passage just reviewed, we certainly see the heavy emphasis on ontological security being maintained. We even see the focus re-narrowed onto the consequences of a specifically modern risk profile for this ontological security. And yet, out of the seven listed elements of the profile, only one – 'the worldwide extension of risk environments' [126] – is significant for its specifically spatial or temporal effects. If ontological security has taken a battering, it seems rather to have been at the hands of a malignant posse of causes, led primarily by industrialism (civil and military), disenchantment (in the Weberian sense) and the contradictory rationality unleashed by the institutionalising of autopoietic systems. The most that could be said of space and time in this assault is that any involvement they did have was due to having fallen under the bad influence of these other causes. And as for the 'front' of the argument, where the transformed conditions of ontological security (whatever their causes) now badly need to start explaining social phenomena (not least those which Giddens has charged classical theory with missing), we cannot even report a collapse for the construction of such explanations has not yet been attempted.

In terms therefore of what chapter 4 needed to achieve, an awful lot now hangs on the last few pages. We are drawn to them by the loudest clarion call yet. Giddens is going to trump Marx and Weber themselves with his own alternative 'big picture' of modernity.

Thickets #3, #4, #5 and #6: The Dialectics of Space and Time

What we have called the 'summative' character of this third part of chapter 4 is evident from the very first paragraph [137], where the earlier series of more partial analyses now gives way to a weighing of competing pictures of modernity as a whole. Weber, we are told, imagined modernity as 'the "steel-hard" cage of bureaucratic rationality' [138]. Marx, by contrast, saw it as 'a monster' – albeit one that might be tamed. 'For these images,' Giddens now proposes, 'we should substitute that of the juggernaut' [139].

Once again, there is something suspicious about this thicket, even when viewed from the outside. Giddens makes a point – in one of only seven footnotes (as opposed to endnotes) in the whole book – of referring the reader to the Hindi origin of the term 'juggernaut', with its connotations of idolatry and human sacrifice. And yet his own brief elaboration of the image in the main text indicates clearly that this is not the operative reference at all. The Hindi *Jagganāth*, presumably, was not 'a runaway engine' which veered at high speed in unpredictable directions, escaping the control of its drivers. The image which actually crystallises as these descriptive brush-strokes are painted in quite obviously relates not to the classical but rather to the vernacular meaning of the term: Giddens is telling us that modernity is like an enormous lorry, whose combined mass and speed generate a momentum which is alternately frightening and exhilarating for those who ride in it and who seek, with very limited controls, to steer its course.

Well, no doubt there is something to be said for this image – even if uncontrollable momentum and unpredictable direction are hardly newly discovered attributes of modernity.[60] But if it is lorries we should be thinking about, why display the (strictly irrelevant) classical reference at this stage? After all, doing so cannot help but remind the reader who has an eye for such things that the image of modernity as a juggernaut, here presented as a fresh alternative to Marx and Weber, has in fact already been used by – who else? – Marx himself.[61] In Marx's case, however, the classical reference fitted exactly the force of what he wanted to say: for a 'civilized' society to slake capital's 'boundless thirst for value' with a stream of unregulated child labour would be to reproduce on a vast scale the very barbarity which the Victorians (with whatever degree of 'orientalist' distortion) imputed to their Indian subjects. England too had its heathen idol, whose worshippers appeased its appetites with human sacrifice.

But there is no point in proceeding further into this thicket, for Giddens himself now tells us that it is empty. No sooner has he introduced the image of the juggernaut than he pushes it aside, in a passage which surely indicates that the nub of the matter is about to be broached:

> The juggernaut of modernity is not all of one piece, and here the imagery lapses, as does any talk of a single path which it runs. It is not an engine made up of integrated machinery, but one in which there is a tensionful, contradictory, push-and-pull of different influences. [139]

That is to say: in order to 'capture the experience of modernity', the replacement image must itself be removed to reveal the 'push and pull of different influences' which its unitary appearance conceals. It is at this point that he makes the programmatic statement which we quoted earlier about the ultimate derivation of 'this view' from 'the dialectics of space and time'. So let us now examine his account of those dialectics, which immediately follows [140–9].

The term 'dialectics' is now used to designate four dimensions of the experience of modern life in which apparently contradictory (or opposite) elements are conjoined in the active, lived experience of individuals. In each case, what '[s]ociologists often suppose' [145] about the experience of modernity is shown to rest on a false dichotomising of these elements, whose actual dialectical resolution cumulatively provides an alternative picture (no longer based on the rigid contrast of *Gemeinschaft* and *Gesellschaft*) of the contemporary world.

Thus the dissolution of 'place' by the disembedding of social relations does not signal the end of community. The same distantiation which renders place phantasmagoric provides simultaneously for the 're-embedding' of social relations via their reinsertion into the new 'time-space contexts' [141] which it unprecedentedly generates. The global may appear to abolish the local; in fact, it now itself becomes the site for the construction of new forms of locality mediated by distantiation.

Second, what applies to the collective experience of community applies equally to the individual experience of intimacy: the impersonality of the *mechanisms* of abstract systems does not define the forms of human interaction which can be mediated by those mechanisms. Telephone systems allow for intimate relationships to be carried on over huge distances. Even the propensity of abstract systems to proliferate technical interactions between unacquainted individuals is not simply the generalising of impersonal behaviour into an anonymous world of 'strangers'; it must also be recognised to involve a vast expansion of the range of possibilities for meeting people and forging personal ties. Intimacy and impersonality therefore are also dialectically related.

Even expertise – that most irresistible invader of the life-world and the public sphere alike – is dialectically compounded with its opposites in the lived world of modernity. Lay individuals, as a simple condition of interaction with abstract systems, develop a practical consciousness of their workings which (however intellectually limited) can become a basis for challenging their operation in various ways. The institutionalised uncertainty at the apex of all reflexive knowledge systems combines with their necessarily fragile dependence on 'access points' on the ground to render technocratic power in principle unstable. The iron cage cannot be locked.

Finally, 'low-probability high-consequence risks' may indeed have 'narcotising effects' which promote 'privatism' in one form or another. Yet, the psychological cost which this entails brings its own necessary qualification to the outcome. Not only does it accumulate a burden of 'existential dread' 'on the level of the unconscious', but also these high-consequence risks which routinely circle the perimeter of lived experience intermittently lunge into the heart of it – in the form of health scares, industrial accidents or political crises. At such points, the scattered elements of personal and social existence are dramatically reconnected, and the psychological repressions of privatism them-selves contribute to the force of the activist engagement which follows.

In conclusion, then, we should not imagine ourselves as trapped in an iron cage, or consumed in the belly of a monster, or even perched on a careering juggernaut. The tissue of our existence does not finally lend itself to any unitary image of this kind. Rather we must see how the touch of human agency, exercised even in the most mundane and unreflective activities of daily life, transforms every disembodied determination into a medium of human purpose, reflexively over-determining it in ways that keep the future forever open.

This is a generous, hopeful and sophisticated argument. We need query it on one issue alone: the issue of what it is explicitly claimed to be demonstrating. In what sense can the four dimensions of this vision be said to comprise – or even to be 'ultimately derived from' – 'dialectics *of space and time*'?

The first of them – displacement and re-embedding – looks at first sight secure enough. Even here, however, there is a problem. The original definition of 'disembedding', which Giddens was at such pains to distinguish from other possible meanings, was 'the "lifting out" of social relations from local contexts of interaction and their restruc-turing across indefinite spans of time-space' [21]. Strictly speaking, therefore, there cannot be a category of 're-embedding' which does not entail a reversal of the process of time-space distantiation. And Giddens' whole argument at this point is that while new forms of local-ity are not unreal, they certainly are phantasmagoric – saturated, that is, with distantiated relations. The actual meaning of 'embedded' has therefore shifted away from its original reference to local spatial enclosure of social causality. It now apparently refers to the (re)insertion of social relations into *any* spatio-temporal matrix, however extensive, which seems to contradict the earlier importance of 'locality' to the definition of 'embedded' (on which, in turn, the spatial force of the metaphor was seen heavily to rest).

Perhaps the way out of this confusion is to say that the category of 'locality' has been dialectically sublated into a new meaning such that it now – paradoxically but legitimately – subsumes distantiation as the mediating condition of modern community. But if so, this can hardly contribute to an argument for the centrality of space and time – if anything, it is their *reduced* significance as barriers to the reconfiguration of social relations which is here underlined.

If there is a difficulty with the first of the four dialectics, it remains nonetheless the only one which provides any materials germane to the case which the four together are supposed to be establishing, or at least illustrating. True, Giddens makes some attempt to weave the second – 'intimacy and impersonality' – into the case. 'The "transformation of intimacy" of which I have spoken', he says, referring us back to the earlier discussion which we have already considered above, 'is contingent upon the very distancing which the disembedding mechanisms bring about' [142]. We know, however, that thicket #1 was empty on just this score: the earlier discussion precisely failed to establish – or even to argue coherently for – any such thing. The offer to construct a spatio-temporal explanation of 'the transformation of intimacy' reverted instead to reliance on a category of institutional differentiation which had itself, even earlier, been rejected as a barrier to appreciating the significance of time-space distantiation. No attempt is made now to provide further evidence. The reader is simply invited to assume that the claim now being made is the next part of a smoothly developing exposition, and rests securely on steps previously established. But we have no grounds for this assumption. On the contrary, having stayed with the argument in the hope that early gaps will be filled by later developments, we are hardly likely to be satisfied when the later developments now refer us back to the earlier sections for substantiation.

Still, if the space-time component of the 'dialectics of space and time' is confused in the first of them, and unsubstantiated in the second, it is barely even mentioned in the third and fourth. With the exception of a late, unsupported suggestion that the contradictory features of modernity should be seen as 'once more reflecting an extraordinary interpolation of the local and the global' [148], there is simply no discussion of space and time even as dimensions within which the last two dialectics are configured, let alone as explanatory elements in understanding how they operate.

As we move into the penultimate chapter, the steady drift of the discussion away from what have supposedly been its central themes picks up speed. Of this chapter, we need only note that it contains a quite remarkable *mélange* of systems theory with vague desiderata for an alternative future (the political obstacles to which are in some cases quite literally wished away).[62] It contains no attempt to provide the long-awaited explanation of those key phenomena whose historical emergence had so pressingly required the supersession of classical social theory. And most importantly for our purposes, there is no longer any significant mention of space, time, ontological security or even time-space distantiation. They have fallen away, disappeared, gone.

And yet they return, one last time, in the diminuendo of the last chapter. This brief (five-page) reprise is made up of two sections: the first considers the question of whether modernity is 'a Western project', while the second mounts a valedictory summary of the overall argument. As this double exercise unfolds, the familiar characters troop back on stage to take their bows – globalisation, risk, space, time, reflexivity and ontological security. But, strange to tell, when we look closely at them, we find that they are not what they were: something has happened to them while they were offstage during the previous chapter.

This first becomes apparent in the opening paragraph of chapter 6. The starting point for answering the question about the Western provenance of modernity is a sudden paring back of the 'organisational complexes [which] are of particular significance' for its institutional definition, from four to two: 'the *nation-state* and *systematic capitalist production*' [174]. These, it is asserted, have 'swept across the world . . . above all because of the power they have generated'. And it is in this context, before any mention of space and time, that 'globalisation' reappears: '[o]ne of the fundamental consequences of modernity'. Globalisation, he says, 'is more than a diffusion of Western institutions across the world' [175]. But is it, at this stage in the argument, still something more than the worldwide spread and uneven development of capitalism and the nation-state? It seems not. For although 'we are speaking here of emergent forms of world interdependence and planetary consciousness', these are developing 'in a global system characterised by great inequalities of wealth and power and cannot but be affected by them'. There is nothing here so far – neither the mental and material interdependence, nor the context of inequality – which cannot be tied back to the spread of the nation-state and capitalism. No wonder 'globalisation' looks different: it has been shorn of all its independent explanatory pretensions. The only additional element which Giddens adds back in at this point is the reflexivity of modern knowledge – and that is linked neither as an additional cause of globalisation, nor as resting on any particular spatio-temporal conditions of its own.

This heavy demotion of globalisation, however, is as nothing compared to the fate which has been prepared for the hapless categories of space and time. That fate arrives on the very last page of the book. 'We are returned here', says Giddens, 'to the theme of time with which this work opened.' What, he wonders, would become of time-space distantiation, disembedding and reflexivity in a genuinely post-modern world? His answer, which would surely raise no eyebrows at all were it not for the direction of the entire antecedent argument, is as follows: '[I]f modern institutions are one day largely transcended, these would also necessarily be fundamentally altered.' The astonished reader might well ask what then was meant by the earlier claim that these 'three sources of the dynamism of modernity' lay in fact '[*b*]*ehind* these institutional clusterings' [63].[63] And indeed a review of that earlier passage does reveal even there a certain ambiguity, according to which the 'sources' are 'involved in as well as conditioned by the institutional dimensions of modernity'. Yet if we take that ambiguity seriously, what becomes of the yet earlier claims for an alternative problematic?

In any case, by the last page of the book, Giddens' mind is made up. Now it is the changing character of time and space which must be 'ultimately derived' from the broader institutional features of particular historical societies. And any 'dialectics of space and time' which we identify must themselves presumably be referred to that more conventional problematic for explanation. In a single blow, the aspiration to a spatio-temporal problematic for social theory has finally been struck down by its own author.

Not for the first time, the shade of Max Weber emerges from the shadows. 'No one knows', he wrote in the concluding paragraphs of his most famous work, 'who will live in this cage in the future, or whether at the end of this tremendous development [of modernity] entirely new prophets will arise, or there will be a great rebirth of old ideas and ideals, or, if neither, mechanised petrification.'[64] Weber allowed himself a brief gasp of horror at this last possibility, before pulling himself up short: 'But this brings us to the world of judgments of value and of faith, with which this purely historical discussion need not be burdened.' 'Whether', echoes Giddens, commenting on his own anticipation of the same post-modern future, 'Whether this would imply a resurgence of religion in some form or other is difficult to say, but there would presumably be a renewed fixity to certain aspects of life that would recall some features of tradition'. And, like Weber, he cuts short his ruminations after a few brief lines: 'With these sorts of reflections, however, we start to dissolve the connection between utopian speculation and realism. And that is further than a study of this type ought to go' [178]. It is a disarmingly modest injunction on which to end the work – albeit one which, one can't help feeling, might usefully have been heeded much, much earlier in the proceedings.

Still, the return of these classical cadences in the closing stanza of the work merely expresses at the surface of the text the more fundamental intellectual adjustment which has occurred beneath. For in the course of these two chapters, implicitly in the first and explicitly in the second, a comprehensive reconfiguration of the argument has been at work. Gradually but unmistakably, *explanans* and *explanandum* have been changing places. And by the end, their initial inversion has itself been fully reversed, bringing us back into line with the pre-existing problematic of modern social theory.

Anthony Giddens has left the building. And, it seems, he has got out just in time. For the overall argument of the book, which he has so hurriedly evacuated at the close, has been teetering dangerously since the opening sections of chapter 4. And we must now observe the concluding spectacle of its comprehensive collapse.

5

Conclusion: The Collapsing Temple of Globalisation Theory

Time and again, in our progress through the early steps of Giddens' argument in *The Consequences of Modernity*, we identified problems of sufficient seriousness as to call into question the logical integrity of anything which followed: the 'springboard' of classical exegesis was insecure; the central claim about space and time led a curious existence – at some points being excluded from the formulation of central propositions, at other points being operationalised with what seemed at the time to be remarkably underwhelming results; even the definition of globalisation seemed caught in a circularity which undermined its credibility at the very point of its original formulation. Yet these misgivings, however strong, could not be conclusive at the time. The argument was not yet fully unfolded. And this, combined with the widely noted 'spiralling' character of Giddens' expository style, meant that they had rather to be referred forward for reconsideration at the end of the process in the light of fuller information. This policy seemed more than justified when Giddens, rounding a further curve on his spiral, carried the argument on to a new level, based on the integration of space, time and ontological security. The intellectual possibilities of the argument seemed genuinely to rise at this point, together with those of a corresponding retrospective resolution of the earlier apparent difficulties. Now conclusive judgement really did have to be deferred until we saw the outcome of his attempt to cash in these possibilities. With the stakes thus raised, and the terms of engagement unambiguously set, we moved on to the fourth chapter, only to find a game of hide and seek which instead raised the evasive character of the whole argument to a new pitch.

Perhaps this is the point at which to note that 'hide and seek' is a smaller version of another game which Giddens has apparently been playing for many years now, with the willing co-operation of not a few of his readers. The larger game is called 'Staying One Step Ahead of the Critics', and is apparently played across successive publications rather than within any one of them.[1] In that game, the demerits of any one volume may be struck out of the account so long as *either* they are addressed in the next one, *or* this next one introduces new ideas which shift the ground sufficiently to change the subject. This rule applies even if the second volume is full of new defects, for the latter are in turn referred to the third volume in the sequence. In this way, the game can be played for many years, avoiding the need for either definitive statements from the author or conclusive judgements by the readers.

Giddens' virtuosity at this game is widely acknowledged to be world-class. And as a move in that wider game, *The Consequences of Modernity* must count as a veritable *coup de main*. For our purpose in this book, however, a different set of rules was required. We wanted to answer the specific question: can the logical foundations of globalisation theory be consolidated at the level of social theory? To help answer this question, we turned to the book most widely assumed to provide that consolidation. And since, ultimately, our engagement was driven by that externally defined question – and not by a negative or positive interest in Giddens *qua* Giddens – the rules we applied were indeed different. They were the *normal* rules of scholarly engagement: does the argument achieve what it sets out to achieve? Is it internally consistent? Is the use of sources reliable?

Perhaps one day Giddens *will* provide a final work which ties up all the loose ends, and reveals how his many earlier publications formed parts of an accumulating and ultimately consistent whole. Then indeed it might be argued that earlier volumes could not be understood, and should not be judged, without reference to the final synthesis. But the globalisation theorists have not waited for that day in order to build their arguments, and neither therefore can we. We must assess the foundations which they have already used, as they actually exist.

A retroactive clarification is thus indeed now in order. But it is clearly not of the kind where we watch the earlier problems disappear as they are reinterpreted in the light of a successful conclusion. On the contrary, we must rather observe the opposite: the self-destructive implications of the final evasion now cascade uncontrollably backwards through the antecedent steps of the argument, knocking their way down through the underlying premises of the theory of time-space distantiation, and passing ultimately beyond Giddens himself to unhinge the shared foundations of globalisation theory as a whole.

For with the argument left finally unsealed, it now becomes significant that Craib charged Giddens with not understanding the writers from whom he has drawn his ideas about 'ontological security'; that Sayer found the representation of Marx's work 'simply laughable', while Turner judged claims made about Weber 'obviously' unsustainable; that Sica drew attention to the subterranean sway of Parsons within the core of structuration theory; and that we ourselves were struck in addition not just by the apparently vulgar reading of Clausewitz, but also by the curious ambiguity in practice of the categorial redefinitions imposed with such apparent purpose on the ideas of writers such as Luhmann and Polanyi.

What we met along the way as a series of unco-ordinated, local criticisms now come together to play a different role: in the absence of any alternative explanation, they start to make retrospective sense of why Giddens' overall problematic was finally unable either to mount successful explanations in the 'front' or to escape the repeated 'return of the repressed' in the rear. Ian Craib's dissection of Giddens' redefinition of 'ontological security' now counts as an explanation of what

before it could only counterfactually predict: that the inbuilt conflation of the social and psychological meanings of trust generates
'notions of ontological security and routine [which] are not sufficient
to carry the theoretical weight that he places on them'; they must
lead instead to explanations which rapidly collapse due to the 'rather
fundamentally oversimplified notion of the individual' with which they
are forced to operate.[2] In a similar way, the critique of classical social
theory, which might have been vindicated had the constructive alternative led anywhere, is now instead confirmed as a misinterpretation
which *explains* why that alternative was unable to escape repeated out-
breaks of 'analytical havoc in the rear'. Indeed, at this stage, even the
critics' cries of 'Parsons! Parsons!', which might have been dismissed
on the way up as mere heckling, now, on the way down, need answering. For it is in fact remarkable how much more can be explained
about *The Consequences of Modernity* (and structuration theory more
generally) by seeing them as a continuation of Parsons, than as representing a break with the latter.

Thus, one by one, the links which earlier allowed the forward movement of the argument are shattered, as the retrospective confirmation
of their unreliability reaches back to connect with the pre-existing
local criticism to render any intervening steps conclusively unsound.

Still, if this is the mechanism of the collapse, the question nonetheless remains: just how far does it go? Our hypothesis all along has been
that, given the use by others of the materials employed in the construction of Giddens' argument, the eventual collapse of that argument
would take far more down with it than Giddens himself. Specifically, we
claimed that the focus on space and time marked the common point of
vulnerability which made Giddens a valid test case for the wider issue of
globalisation theory. Can we now substantiate this claim?

This is such an important question that it is worth breaking it down
into its component elements so as to be sure of the maximum clarity
in our answer. We can do this by working our way through three sub-
questions. First, does the general mechanism of backward collapse
which we have identified apply specifically to the spatio-temporal

theme in *Consequences*? Second, if so, can it be shown that Giddens' problems in this book really do derive from the central role accorded to space and time? And finally, even if it can, how far can this result be generalised from the failings of one author to the liabilities of an entire intellectual discourse – namely globalisation theory?

As to the first question, the answer is straightforward enough. Working our way backwards: it is the concluding failure of the 'dialectics of space and time' even to *be* dialectics of space and time (let alone to generate convincing spatio-temporal explanations of social phenomena) which brings to an end the attempt to reground the overall argument in a spatio-temporal definition of ontological security. And the rescue having now miscarried, the yet earlier claims made for abstract systems have no defence against the criticisms lodged at the time: that is to say, the 'flattening out' of different abstract systems around their shared spatio-temporal extensiveness can no longer be defended by the hope those common spatio-temporal features will at some future point be shown to be more causally significant for modernity than are the differentiated social contents of the systems which have been effaced. This in turn undermines the virtue of providing a spatio-temporal analysis of modern institutions. And because the problem there clearly relates not to a descriptive use of these categories, but specifically to their explanatory use as an alternative to the explanatory categories of Marx and Weber, the collapse is transmitted further and further back, crashing down through the critique of classical social theory, and onto the foundations of time-space distantiation itself, whose basic propositions, it is now clear, were always unable to sustain the weight of the arguments which were erected above them.

Our second question can receive an equally unambiguous answer. On the one hand, if we take Giddens at his word, then the centrality of the spatio-temporal theme to the entire argument is simply beyond dispute. The whole point, after all, of the 'fresh characterisation of modernity' was to provide a reinterpretation of contemporary society in the light of spatio-temporal transformations which now required the simultaneous installation of 'globalisation' at the empirical apex of social explanation, and 'the problematic of time-space distantiation' at its theoretical base. And, as we have seen, Giddens' rhetorical insistence on this definition of his project remains undiminished almost to the very end.

On the other hand, the really decisive point here does not depend on his intentions, declared or otherwise. For if we now work our way forwards through the stages of the argument, we can see for ourselves that almost all the key displacements which confound its logical coherence occur at nodal points where the pitch for spatio-temporal categories has to be made. It is the insistence on *counterposing* a spatio-temporal definition of 'disembedding' to its traditional usage (rather than simply exploring the undeniable spatio-temporal implications of the latter) which lumbers Giddens with a category which cannot help but change meanings again when it is applied to 'the transformation of intimacy'. Yet such a counterposing *is* what is entailed by the scale of the claims he has earlier made for time-space distantiation as an alternative problematic for social theory. Similarly, it is the final failure of the regrounding of ontological security in space and time to produce any explanation which eventually brings the whole thing crashing down. Yet, by half-way through *Consequences*, such an effort *is* the only direction in which Giddens can go if he is to resolve under the sign of space and time the contradictions which have accumulated so far.

In short, it is the enterprise itself that forces him onto these rocky paths. It confronts him with one impossible task after another. This tyrannical muse of space and time grants, it seems, only one consolation to the servant who labours so tirelessly on her behalf: miraculously, he is shielded from any awareness of the ultimate futility of the tasks. And the argument which appears to us to stumble at every turn feels itself to be soaring.

On then, finally, to the third question: the argument may have collapsed; we might even infer from the direction of the collapse that the spatio-temporal element formed the central crack running through the entire structure; yet how far can these results seriously be generalised to the whole discourse of globalisation theory?

The question leads us all the way back to our opening reflections on exactly what is logically entailed by claims – any claims – for a new, spatio-temporal problematic for social theory. We suggested first that globalisation theory, in the sense in which we have defined it, was tied to such claims. Without them, the term itself would revert to a purely descriptive role, and the categories of space and time could not assume the central explanatory significance which is urged for them. We saw in our discussions of Scholte and Walker that the globalisation theorists themselves, far from contesting this suggestion, seem happy in their different ways to embrace it. Consequently, there remains only one way in which the discourse as a whole can now avoid the falling masonry: and that is to claim that a better architect might yet build a sounder structure on the same foundations.

Who could deny that Giddens has brought his own strengths and weaknesses as an individual writer to the intellectual challenge of globalisation theory? Other writers have gone about it in different ways. There are many nuances to be drawn between Scholte's 'supraterritoriality', Walker's 'temporal accelerations' and Giddens' 'time-space distantiation'. And we cannot predict what new approaches will be taken in the future. There is, however, one thing which we can predict with complete certainty: every one of these approaches, whatever its form, will have to face a common requirement which derives not from the approach itself but from the claims which it is attempting to substantiate.

If there really is to be an alternative, spatio-temporal problematic for social theory – and not simply another middle-range hypothesis operating within the known world of existing theoretical assumptions – then there is a limit to how far this new problematic can pick and choose where its explanatory propositions apply. It is compelled, by its own self-definition, to compete with existing problematics on the centreground of social explanation – or to convince us that the centreground lies elsewhere. It was this requirement which actually defeated Giddens' enterprise, as he failed first to occupy and then to shift that centreground. Scholte, wisely, did not try to meet it. Walker found its implications 'exceptionally difficult'. It is, at any rate, not a requirement that Giddens faces alone.

Admittedly, the example of *Consequences* appears at first sight to be rather extreme: not only do the very 'institutional dimensions of modernity' escape spatio-temporal definition; but often (as in the case of 'the transformation of intimacy') spatio-temporal explanations are proclaimed where they are not in fact occurring. Extreme as it may appear, however, it is not at all unrepresentative. On the contrary, because these problems are rooted ultimately in the general case, and precisely not in any individual approach to it, they resurface automatically within any attempt to substantiate that case. They express, in short, the inner contradiction of the idea itself.

Consider, as a last example, the parallel instance of Zygmunt Bauman. Writing of the erosion of the nation-state by transnational forces, he tells us:

> Its causes are not fully understood; it cannot be exactly predicted even if the causes are known; and it certainly cannot be prevented from happening even if predicted.[3]

Well, fine, but this is hardly fighting talk from a brave new problematic which began by loudly announcing itself as the basis for a comprehensive reinterpretation of world history, no less. And when he tells us on the same page that the collective demiurge of this process – comprised of the same transnational forces – is itself 'blurred in the mist of mystery', one feels compelled to ask: on what intellectual basis, then, is this new problematic recommending itself? Before one can find an answer to this, however, the central claims are, just as with Giddens, overtaken by analytical havoc in the rear. Although these claims retain their rhetorical sound and fury, the overwhelming analytical significance of space and time gradually recedes within them. And as 'the mist of mystery' clears, the argument comes to rest on a different, and altogether more familiar, shore. The spatio-temporal transformations which we call 'globalisation' are, it turns out, 'triggered (though by no means determined) by the radical leap in the technology of speed'.[4] What actually drives them is their use by 'capital' to secure, extend and obscure the exploitative and distributive mechanisms through which inequalities of wealth and power are reproduced in the contemporary world. And since Bauman does not offer to use space and time to explain the mechanisms themselves (but only their invisibility and their successful insulation from effective protest), one must assume that the intellectual horns of the new problematic, so vigorously thrust forward at the start of the book, have been well and truly drawn in by the close.

And wisely so. For all the evidence now seems to point to a single, simple conclusion: the intellectual requirement we have been discussing is itself the ultimate source of the problem. It unavoidably pushes the categories of space and time into a role which they cannot be imagined to fulfil. That being so, even the arguments over whether globalisation theory is right or wrong start to lose their purchase. Hamstrung at a deeper, definitional level, the discourse would be unable even to rise to a coherent propositional statement without incurring the charge of a category error.

And for the argument built on a category error, a special kind of intellectual judgement is reserved, reminiscent of Richard Cobden's verdict on balance of power theory:

> It is not a fallacy, a mistake, an imposture – it is an undescribed, indescribable, incomprehensible nothing; mere words, conveying to the mind not ideas, but sounds like those equally barren syllables which our ancestors put together for the purpose of puzzling themselves about words, in the shape of *Prester John*, or the *philosopher's stone*![5]

Cobden, in fact, was mistaken about the balance of power. And we may yet be mistaken about globalisation theory. But if so, this now needs to be shown. The wild, speculative debut of this discourse cannot go on forever. At some point, the normal rules of intellectual coherence must re-assert themselves. And when they do, the message for globalisation theory will be the same as for every other grand theory which has strutted and turned on the stage of social science: substance, soon, or silence.

1990; the cartographic studies of David Woodward (for example, 'Reality, Symbolism, Time, and Space in Medieval World Maps', *Annals of the Association of American Geographers*, 75 (4), 1985), and so on.

14. Joseph Needham, for example, challenged – or at any rate qualified very heavily – the notion that classical Chinese civilisation did not know the progressive, unilinear conceptions of time conventionally attributed uniquely to the modern West. See 'Time and Eastern Man' in his *The Grand Titration: Science and Society in East and West*, London 1969.

15. In addition to the works already cited, the *locus classicus* for studies of the interrelation of temporal with other social forms in the process of historical change surely remains E.P. Thompson's 'Time, Work-Discipline and Industrial Capitalism', *Past and Present*, 38, 1967 (reprinted in *Customs in Common*, London 1991). But see also, for a more recent example of the genre, M. French Smith's 'Bloody Time and Bloody Scarcity: Capitalism, Authority, and the Transformation of Temporal Experience in a Papua New Guinea Village', *American Ethnologist*, 9, 1982, 503–18.

16. See for example, B. Anderson, *Imagined Communities: Reflections on the Origin and Spread of Nationalism*, 2nd edn, London 1991.

17. N. Poulantzas, *State, Power, Socialism*, London 1978, especially chapter 4.

18. Sack, *Human Territoriality*, p. 223.

19. Shakespeare, *King Lear*, Act II, Scene IV.

20. C. Wright Mills, *The Sociological Imagination*, Oxford 1959. For an attempt to relate Mills' arguments directly to the concerns of IR theory, see J. Rosenberg, 'The International Imagination: IR Theory and Classic Social Analysis', *Millennium*, 23 (1), Spring 1994.

21. J.A. Scholte, 'Globalisation: Prospects for a Paradigm Shift', in M. Shaw, ed., *Politics and Globalisation*, London 1999, p. 18.

22. Waters, *Globalization*, p. 27.

23. Ibid., p. 28

24. For an overview of these works, see I. Clark, *Globalization and International Relations Theory*, Oxford 1999.

25. James Rosenau, cited in Waters, *Globalization*, p. 30.

26. Cambridge 1993.

27. Z. Bauman, *Intimations of Postmodernity*, London 1992, pp. 59–65.

28. 'The story is told of you.'

2. SCHOLTE'S FOLLY

1. J.A. Scholte, *Globalization: A Critical Introduction*, Basingstoke 2000, p. xiv.

2. The quotations can be found on pages 315 and 5 respectively.

3. Archer, cited in Scholte, *Globalization*, p. 15.

4. Ibid., pp. 15–16.

5. Ibid., p. 43.

6. Ibid., p. 137.

7. Ibid., p. 46.

8. Ibid., p. 5.

9. Ibid., p. 47.

10. Ibid., p. 49.

11. Ibid., p. 50.

12. The quotations used in this paragraph are all taken from ibid., pp. 50–6.

13. Ibid., p. 14.

14. J.A. Scholte, 'Globalisation: Prospects for a Paradigm Shift', in M. Shaw, ed., *Politics and Globalisation*, London 1999, pp. 9, 20, 19 and 21.

15. A fine, though not up to date, selection of readings on the Thirty Years War can be found in T. Rabb, ed., *The Thirty Years' War: Problems of Motive, Extent, and Effect*, Boston 1964. C.V. Wedgwood's classic, *The Thirty Years War*, London 1938, remains as readable as ever.

16. Commenting in 1948 on the newly drafted UN Charter, Leo Gross observed that 'the Peace of Westphalia may be said to continue its sway over political man's mind as the *ratio scripta* that it was held to be of yore.' See 'The Peace of Westphalia 1648–1948', *The American Journal of International Law*, 42, 1948, p. 21.

17. A translation of the treaty can be found in G. Symcox, ed., *War, Diplomacy, and Imperialism, 1618–1763: Selected Documents*, London 1974.

18. For examples of these, see, respectively, S. Krasner, 'Westphalia and All That', in J. Goldstein and R. Keohane, eds, *Ideas and Foreign Policy: Beliefs, Institutions and Political Change*, New York 1993, and J. Rosenberg, *The Empire of Civil Society: A Critique of the Realist Theory of International Relations*, London 1994, chapter 5.

19. *Review of International Studies*, 24, Special Issue, December 1998, pp. 220, 221 and 242. To be fair, it should be noted that while the journal's table of contents lists the title as I have cited it, the article itself appears under the following: 'The End of the Old Order? Globalization and the Prospects for World Order'. The phenomenon of the 'folly' seems in fact to be a general characteristic of the so-called 'transformationalist' school of globalisation theory.

20. D. Held, A. McGrew, D. Goldblatt and J. Perraton, *Global Transformations: Politics, Economics, Culture*, Cambridge 1999, pp. 37–9.

21. All the quotations in this paragraph come from Scholte, *Globalization*, p. 57.

22. Reprinted in A. Shaw, ed., *Great Britain and the Colonies 1815–1865*, London 1970. (Originally published in *Economic History Review*, Second Series, VI (I), 1953.)

23. Ibid., pp. 142 and 159.

24. G. Stedman Jones, 'The History of US Imperialism', in R. Blackburn, ed., *Ideology in Social Science: Readings in Critical Social Theory*, London 1972, pp. 209 and 212.

25. For discussion of and figures relating to all of these, see E. Wolf, *Europe and the People Without History*, Berkeley, CA, 1982, chapter 9, and E.J. Hobsbawm, *Industry and Empire*, Harmondsworth 1968, especially chapter 7.

26. Scholte, *Globalization*, p. 57.

27. *History of Bourgeois Perception*, Brighton 1982, chapter 4.

28. K. Marx, *Capital*, Volume I, trans. B. Fowkes, Harmondsworth 1976, p. 925.

29. Scholte, *Globalization*, p. 59.

30. In fact, according to Marx, he invented nothing at all, but was rather 'the greatest thief of other people's inventions'. See *Capital*, Volume I, pp. 549–50.

31. See K. Bourne, *The Foreign Policy of Victorian England 1830–1902*, Oxford 1970, pp. 269–70.

32. The quotations from Scholte in this paragraph come from *Globalization*, pp. 143, 74, 60 and 136 respectively.

33. K. Marx, *Readings from Karl Marx*, ed. D. Sayer, London 1989, p. 62. In the Nicolaus translation of the *Grundrisse*, the relevant passage can be found on page 138.

34. D. Sayer, *Capitalism and Modernity: An Excursus on Marx and Weber*, London 1991, p. 56. Sayer continues: 'Marx is arguing, not that capitalism causes distinctively modern forms of sociation to arise, but that it is itself a distinctly modern form of sociation.'

35. For a clear and more detailed exposition of the points which follow, see ibid., chapter 2. Sayer produced an even fuller analysis in an earlier journal article. See 'The Critique of Politics and Political Economy: Capitalism, Communism and the State in Marx's Writings of the mid-1840s', *Sociological Review*, 33 (2), 1985.

36. Marx, *Readings from Karl Marx*, p. 123.

37. Ibid., p. 116. For an attempt to explain the earlier historical examples of the 'abstraction of the political' in classical Greece and Renaissance Italy, which seem at first to contradict this claim, see Rosenberg, *Empire*, chapter 3.

38. Marx, *Readings from Karl Marx*, p. 116.

39. Ibid., pp. 123–4.
40. Ibid., p. 124.
41. For a fuller exposition of these points, see Rosenberg, *Empire*, chapter 5.
42. N. Poulantzas, *State, Power, Socialism*, London 1978, p. 95.
43. In the definition of the Westphalian model provided by Held and his fellow authors, only one of its seven elements makes any reference at all to any non-state dimension of society – and even that is only for the purpose of registering its legal disconnection from the business of geopolitics: 'Responsibility for cross-border wrongful acts is a "private matter" concerning only those affected.' *Global Transformations*, p. 38.
44. Poulantzas, *State, Power, Socialism*, p. 106.
45. Scholte, *Globalization*, p. 58.
46. Ibid., p. 60.
47. Poulantzas, *State, Power, Socialism*, p. 100.
48. Ibid., p. 106.
49. Ibid., p. 99.

3. ROB WALKER: PHILOSOPHICAL BACKSTOP?

1. 'Science as a Vocation', in *From Max Weber*, ed. H. Gerth and C. Wright Mills, London 1948, p. 145.
2. D. Held, A. McGrew, D. Goldblatt and J. Perraton, *Global Transformations: Politics, Economics, Culture*, Cambridge 1999, p. 50.
3. G. Youngs, *International Relations in a Global Age: A Conceptual Challenge*, Cambridge 1999, p. 76, emphasis added.
4. R.B.J. Walker, *Inside/Outside: International Relations as Political Theory*, Cambridge 1993, p. 2.
5. R.B.J. Walker, 'International Relations and the Concept of the Political', in K. Booth and S. Smith, eds, *International Relations Theory Today*, Cambridge 1995, p. 322.

6. I refer to the following statement (ibid., p. 7), which I have italicised and annotated (in square brackets) in order to illustrate the point: '*Part* [but only part] of my aim is to *explore* [but not necessarily endorse] *some* [but only some] of the *implications* [not the substance] of recent *attempts* [I won't say they've succeeded] to *canvass* [rather than establish] the *possibility* [let alone the substantive validity] of an explicitly critical attitude within the theory of international relations.' The remarkable quality of this sentence lies in the fact that the closer the reader approaches to the definitive phrase 'explicitly critical attitude', the further Walker himself has been distanced from it by the accumulating layers of qualification.

7. Walker, *Inside/Outside*, p. 161.

8. 'International Relations', p. 313; *Inside/Outside*, pp. 17, 157; 'International Relations', p. 313; *Inside/Outside*, pp. 21, 162, 103.

9. Walker, 'International Relations', p. 314.

10. Walker, *Inside/Outside*, pp. 2, 8, 155, 158, 16.

11. Ibid., pp. 9, 5, 6, and Walker, 'International Relations', p. 309.

12. Walker, 'International Relations', p. 310.

13. Walker, *Inside/Outside*, p. 157.

14. Ibid.

15. Ibid., p. 21.

16. Walker, 'International Relations', p. 320.

17. See Walker, *Inside/Outside*, pp. 113–14.

18. Ibid., p. 60.

19. Ibid., p. 27.

20. Ibid., p. 127.

21. Ibid., p. 129.

22. Ibid., p. 82.

23. A difficulty noted by Lene Hansen. See 'R.B.J. Walker and International Relations: Deconstructing a Discipline', in I. Neumann and O. Wæver, eds, *The Future of International Relations: Masters in the Making*, London 1997, p. 322.

24. Walker, *Inside/Outside*, p. 45.

25. Walker, 'International Relations', p. 319.
26. Ibid., p. 320.
27. Walker, *Inside/Outside*, p. 46.
28. Walker, 'International Relations', p. 312.
29. Walker, *Inside/Outside*, p. 6.
30. Walker, 'International Relations', p. 320.
31. Walker, *Inside/Outside*, p. 14.
32. Ibid., p. 14.
33. Ibid., p. 89.
34. Ibid., pp. 149-50.
35. Ibid., p. 149.
36. Ibid., p. 45.
37. Ibid., p. 46.
38. Ibid., p. 129.
39. Walker, 'International Relations', p. 306.
40. Walker, *Inside/Outside*, p. 177.
41. Ibid., p. 176.
42. Ibid., p. 177.
43. M. Wight, 'Why is There No International Theory?', in H. Butterfield and M. Wight, eds, *Diplomatic Investigations*, London 1966.
44. Walker, *Inside/Outside*, p. 177.
45. Ibid., p. 158.
46. Ibid., p. 63.
47. See, for example, the statement on page 153: 'The limits within which accounts of democratic possibilities are constrained are the limits of the particular community set among a system of other particular communities.'
48. Ibid., p. 78.
49. See ibid., pp. 136 and 173-4 respectively.
50. Ibid., p. 136.
51. Ibid., p. 172.
52. Ibid., p. 173.
53. Ibid., p. 2.

54. Ibid., p. 3.
55. Ibid., pp. 46 and 155.
56. Ibid., p. 143.
57. Ibid., p. 3.
58. Ibid., p. 157.
59. See the section entitled 'After Eternity' in Walker, 'International Relations', pp. 322–4.
60. B. Anderson, *Imagined Communities: Reflections on the Origin and Spread of Nationalism*, London 1983. Page references to this text apply to the second edition, London 1991.
61. Ibid., p. 36.
62. Ibid., p. 11.
63. For the classic interpretation of Weber's *oeuvre* (and indeed Marx's too) in terms of its philosophical anthropology, see K. Löwith, *Max Weber and Karl Marx*, ed. T. Bottomore and W. Outhwaite, London 1982.
64. 'Max Weber and Ernest Gellner', in P. Anderson, *A Zone of Engagement*, London 1992, p. 205. There is in fact an interesting parallel with Walker here. '[I]s there anything missing in Walker's account of state sovereignty?' asks Lene Hansen. 'The most important omission seems to be his neglect of nation.' See 'R.B.J. Walker and International Relations', p. 332.
65. Walker, *Inside/Outside*, p. 129.
66. Anderson, *Imagined Communities*, p. 24.
67. 'What', asked Poulantzas, 'makes possible the emergence of a specific space whose contours designate an inside and an outside?' Exploring how 'the capitalist State has the peculiarity of reserving social space and time for itself', he went on to define political *'frontiers in the modern sense of the term'* as 'limits capable of being shifted along a serial and discontinuous loom which everywhere fixes *insides* and *outsides*'. It was, he argued, precisely the state which marked out 'the frontiers of what thereby becomes the inside of an outside'. And so on. See *State, Power, Socialism*, London 1978, pp. 96, 99, 104 and 106 respectively.

68. K. Marx, *Grundrisse*, trans. M. Nicolaus, Harmondsworth 1973, p. 164.

69. D. Lowe, *History of Bourgeois Perception*, Brighton 1982, p. 59.

70. See especially a footnote on page 179, where he writes of a statement by Lord Curzon: 'Foucault could not have said it better.'

71. F. Nietzsche, *The Gay Science*, trans. W. Kaufmann, New York 1974, p. 182.

72. Walker, *Inside/Outside*, p. 164.

73. Ibid., p. 151.

74. M. Donelan, 'The Political Theorists and International Theory', in M. Donelan, ed., *The Reason of States: A Study in International Political Theory*, London 1978, p. 77.

75. Ibid., p. 79.

76. Ibid., p. 83.

77. Hansen, 'R.B.J. Walker and International Relations', p. 331.

78. R.B.J. Walker, 'On Pedagogical Responsibility: A Response to Roy Jones', *Review of International Studies*, 20, 1994, p. 319. Jones' review, published in the same issue, was entitled 'The Responsibility to Educate'.

79. Marx, *Grundrisse*, p. 86.

80. Ibid.

81. Ibid., p. 88.

82. Ibid., p. 87.

83. Ibid., p. 106.

84. Ibid., p. 83.

85. Ibid., p. 85.

86. Ibid.

87. Ibid. I have stayed with the Nicolaus translation here because it strikes me as the one which renders the logic of the point most concisely – even if it makes it appear that the object switches from 'language' back to 'production' before the formulation is completed. Other translations make it clearer that the case of language is invoked as *methodologically analogous* to that of production, rather than (as the Nicolaus version might imply)

substantively derivative of it. See for alternative translations: David McLellan's *Marx's Grundrisse*, St Albans 1973, p. 28; Terrell Carver's *Karl Marx: Texts on Method*, Oxford 1975, p. 51; and Derek Sayer's *Readings from Karl Marx*, London 1989, pp. 35–6.

88. These words – *Grundrisse*, p. 88 – comprise the title of this second section.

89. Ibid., p. 99.

90. Ibid., p. 85.

91. Ibid.

92. See ibid., p. 472.

93. Marx to Kugelmann, 11 July 1868, in Karl Marx and Friedrich Engels, *Correspondence 1846–1895*, ed. and trans. D. Torr, London 1934, p. 246.

94. I owe this formulation, and indeed this turn of the argument, to Simon Bromley.

95. See for an especially clear example of this, Herbert Butterfield's 'The Tragic Element in Modern International Conflict', in his *History and Human Relations*, London 1951.

96. The representative figure here is of course Kenneth Waltz, especially in his *Theory of International Politics*, New York 1979.

97. It might help at this point to note the following. Marx's category of 'production in general' is not the same thing as, and does not even presuppose, the materialist conception of history. The latter hypothesis is logically subsequent to, and not contained in, the general abstraction of production. Similarly, our general abstraction of the international carries no claim about the relative causal weight of the international in any social order. Thus the natural suspicion that a 'problematic of the international' is somehow incompatible with historical materialism appears to be unfounded. This can be confirmed by reviewing some of the other general abstractions which Marx found it useful to develop. Thus in chapter 7 of Volume I of *Capital* (trans. B. Fowkes, Harmondsworth 1976) the general abstraction 'labour' is initially constructed without any reference to its social dimension, on

which the theory of historical materialism insists. This is later followed by a general abstraction of 'co-operation' (chapter 13) which embodies no materialist explanatory premise. The same is true of a general abstraction of society invoked in a letter to Annenkov of 28 December 1846: 'What is society, whatever its form may be? The product of men's reciprocal activity.' (See Marx and Engels, *Correspondence 1846–1895*, p. 7.)

98.   J. Rosenberg, *The Empire of Civil Society: A Critique of the Realist Theory of International Relations*, London 1994, p. 46.

99.   Marx, *Capital*, Volume I, p. 493. In this case the example being discussed was that of 'machinery'.

100. Ibid., p. 727.

101. For the following, see Walker, *Inside/Outside*, pp. 65–6.

102. 'That slavery can be justified by such a convention', says Aristotle of this practice, 'is a principle against which a number of jurists bring what may be called an "indictment of illegality".' Aristotle's subsequent comparison of the doctrine of 'natural slavery' (which applies to barbarians) with the possible grounds for justifying the enslavement of citizens captured in war is fascinating; but it confirms the routine occurrence of the latter nevertheless. And the later discussion of the nature of different forms of rule – over slaves, over non-slave dependants, and over other (free) citizens – keeps the distinction 'clear cut' indeed: '[T]he fact remains [unlike in the other two cases] that the rule is primarily exercised with a view to the master's interest, and only incidentally with a view to that over the slave.' See *The Politics of Aristotle*, trans. E. Barker, Oxford 1946, pp. 14–17 and 111–12.

4. GIDDENS' *CONSEQUENCES OF MODERNITY*: SOCIOLOGICAL FOUNDATIONS?

1.   A. Giddens, *Capitalism and Modern Social Theory*, Cambridge 1971.

2. Cambridge 1985.

3. Whether this reflects a genuine intellectual synthesis, rather than an 'infinitely stretchable' indeterminacy, at the heart of Giddens' work is a recurrent theme of the critical literature. See, for example, Stewart Clegg's entertaining and illuminating analysis of Giddens' publishing success in terms of intellectual 'product management': 'How to Become an Internationally Famous British Social Theorist', republished in C. Bryant and D. Jary, eds, *Anthony Giddens: Critical Assessments* (4 vols), Volume I, London 1997. Admirers and critics alike owe a considerable debt to Bryant and Jary for this enormously useful compilation.

4. See in particular his 'Glocalization: Time-Space and Homogeneity-Heterogeneity', in M. Featherstone, S. Lash and R. Robertson, eds, *Global Modernities*, London 1995, and his *Globalization: Social Theory and Global Culture*, London 1992. The latter contains, among other interesting materials, a sharp and penetrating critique of *The Consequences of Modernity*.

5. Despite Albrow's helpful practice of inserting an explanatory tag at the head of each of the sub-sections of *The Global Age* (Cambridge 1996), I have not yet succeeded in putting these 95 parts together in such a way as to be able to assess the overall argument he is making.

6. D. Held, A. McGrew, D. Goldblatt and J. Perraton, *Global Transformations: Politics, Economics and Culture*, Cambridge 1999. Rosenau's assessment is reproduced on the front cover. In this work (as also in Malcolm Waters' *Globalization*, London 1995), Giddens is cited more frequently than any other author. Giddens himself describes this volume as 'the most comprehensive introduction to the subject of globalisation produced to date'. (See A. Giddens, *Runaway World: How Globalisation is Reshaping Our Lives*, London 1999, p. 84.)

7. The book also develops an effective running critique of postmodernism, not reviewed in the pages below, arguing that its

preoccupations reflect the radical epistemological and phenomenological consequences of 'high' modernity itself.

8. A. Giddens, *The Consequences of Modernity*, Cambridge 1990, p. 1. In the pages which follow, all numbers in square brackets indicate page references to this text.

9. 'I wanted to use the study of the "classics" to provide a springboard for other, related endeavours.' 'Structuration Theory and Sociological Analysis', in J. Clark, C. Modgil and S. Modgil, eds, *Anthony Giddens: Consensus and Controversy*, Basingstoke 1990, p. 298.

10. K. Marx, *Grundrisse*, Harmondsworth 1973, trans. M. Nicolaus, p. 158. 'Objective dependence' is Nicolaus' rendering of the phrase elsewhere translated as 'dependence mediated by things'.

11. See, for example D. Sayer, *Capitalism and Modernity: An Excursus on Marx and Weber*, London 1991, p. 14: '[W]hen reflecting on the course of human history at this level of generality, Marx simply conflates as his "first stage" *all* precapitalist social formations.' Giddens himself is well aware of the opening for a non-evolutionist reading of Marx: 'I think the importance of Marx is really to point up the differences between capitalism and pre-existing societies and not to try and compress them all into some overall scheme of evolutionary change.' J. Bleicher and M. Featherstone, 'Historical Materialism Today: An Interview with Anthony Giddens', reproduced in Bryant and Jary, eds, *Anthony Giddens: Critical Assessments*, Volume I, p. 24.

12. Or as Sayer puts it: 'A sense of the fundamental novelty of the world taking visible shape in the nineteenth century is in one way or another a staple of all "classical" sociologies. . . . [M]odernity can be argued to be *the* object of enquiry which first grounded the establishment of sociology as an independent academic discipline.' (*Capitalism and Modernity*, p. 11.) Elsewhere, Sayer describes Giddens' criticism of Marx on this count as 'simply laughable'. See his 'Reinventing the Wheel: Anthony Giddens,

Karl Marx and Social Change', in Clark et al., eds, *Anthony Giddens: Consensus and Controversy*, p. 242.

13. M. Berman, *All That is Solid Melts into Air*, London 1983, p. 19.

14. Ibid., p. 24. Giddens also suggests in passing that Marx did not give due weight to the 'sombre side' of modernity, and that this is evidenced by his belief that the contradictions of the present contained within themselves the possibility of 'a more humane social system'. And this is also peculiar – not just because it is unclear in what other terms one is supposed to think of the future without indulging either a rootless utopianism or a despairing paralysis, but also because exactly the same procedure is adopted by Giddens himself in the penultimate chapter of *The Consequences of Modernity*.

15. See, for example, Giddens, *The Nation-State and Violence*. There, indeed, the theory of time-space distantiation is used to argue for the overwhelming importance of a bounded entity: '[T]he modern state, as nation-state, becomes in many respects the pre-eminent form of power container, as a territorially bounded . . . administrative unity.' And Marx is castigated, along with 'liberal sociology', for lacking 'a systematic interpretation of the rise of the territorially bounded nation-state and its association with military power' (pp. 13, 26).

16. For a brief interrogation of Giddens' misrepresentation of Weber in *The Consequences of Modernity*, see B. Turner, 'Weber, Giddens and Modernity', reproduced in Bryant and Jary, eds, *Anthony Giddens: Critical Assessments*, Volume IV. Turner observes, *inter alia*, that 'it is obviously the case that Weber did not operate with a conception of "society" as "the nation-state". . . . [H]e specifically said that, if he had become a sociologist at all, it was to expunge reified concepts like society and nation from the vocabulary of science' (p. 38).

17. The argument for this is given at length in '"Objectivity" in Social Science and Social Policy', reprinted in M. Weber, *The Methodology of the Social Sciences*, trans. and ed. E. Shills and H.

Finch, New York 1949. The definition of social science as a cultural science appears on page 67.

18. *The Protestant Ethic and the Spirit of Capitalism*, trans. T. Parsons, London 1984, p. 182.

19. Weber, '"Objectivity" in Social Science', p. 57.

20. 'Further Adventures of Charisma', in *Language and Power: Exploring Political Cultures in Indonesia*, Ithaca, NY, and London 1990.

21. Giddens draws the phrase 'socialised nature' [127] from Ulrich Beck's *Risk Society* (trans. M. Ritter, London 1992). Beck's penchant for serving up old wine in new bottles is apparently as uncontrollable as that of Giddens himself, and nowhere more so than in his proclamation in that work of '*the end of the antithesis between nature and society.*' (Ibid., p. 80.) 'At the end of the twentieth century,' he says, 'nature *is* society and society is also "*nature*". Anyone who continues to speak of nature as non-society is speaking in terms from a different century, which no longer capture our reality.' (Ibid., p. 81.) What on earth then does Beck think that Marx *meant* by the phrase 'materialist conception of history'? The fact that Beck's bibliography includes Marx's early writings only makes the question even more pressing. For it was there that Marx already advanced the notion of 'humanised nature', rejected any antithesis of nature and society, and wrote instead of '[n]ature as it comes into being in human history – in the act of creation of human society'. See Marx, *Early Writings*, trans. R. Livingstone and G. Benton, Harmondsworth 1975, pp. 353 and 355.

22. For a discussion of this earlier role, see A. Sica, 'The California–Massachusetts Strain in Structuration Theory', reproduced in Bryant and Jary, eds, *Anthony Giddens: Critical Assessments*, Volume I, pp. 292ff.

23. See Giddens, *Central Problems in Social Theory*, London 1979, pp. 237 and 244.

24. Giddens, *Capitalism and Modern Social Theory*, p. 23.

25. Ibid., p. 247.
26. A. Giddens, *The Constitution of Society*, Cambridge 1984, pp. xv and xxix. The latter quotation reflects a mid-point intellectually as well as chronologically in the distance travelled by Giddens over the two decades before the publication of *The Consequences of Modernity*. If it does not yet approach the later full-blown claim that Marx was a social evolutionist, it has nonetheless already departed considerably from his position in 1971, when Giddens was reluctant even to associate Engels' term 'historical material-ism' with Marx on the grounds that 'it perhaps suggests a greater degree of theoretical closure than Marx would be willing to admit of his studies of history'. See fn. 18 on p. 4 of *Capitalism and Modern Social Theory*.
27. This is all the more remarkable since Giddens shows an aware-ness of past instances of this. He states, for example, that the Second International was 'a context which transmitted [*sic*] Marx's original conception into one which appeared much more as the direct *expression* of the main intellectual trends of the nineteenth century than as a critical analysis and an attempt to supersede them'. See *Capitalism and Modern Social Theory*, p. 244.
28. The idea of a 'return' of Parsonian categories may actually under-state the case. In a remarkable exercise in detective exegesis, Sica has argued that Giddens' 'authorial strategy of deflection and feinting has tricked' many of his readers into seeing him as 'a child of the left . . . [located] firmly within a European family tree of intellectuals'. ('The California–Massachusetts Strain', pp. 302–3.) In fact, says Sica, Giddens should more accurately be designated as an American thinker; for the unacknowledged roots of structuration theory, concealed by a false trail of 'redefinitional ingenuity', lie in an unoriginal fusion of ethnomethodology, sym-bolic interactionism and systems theory: '[T]hroughout his later theorising, whenever the question of self/society appears, one can hear the unnamed echo of ideas long popular in southern

California, and even important remnants of others dreamed up in Cambridge, Massachusetts.' (Ibid., pp. 302–3.)

29. Z. Bauman, *Globalization: The Human Consequences*, Cambridge 1998, p. 14.

30. K. Marx, *Capital*, Volume I, trans. B. Fowkes, Harmondsworth 1976, p. 187.

31. Ibid., pp. 187–8.

32. I have been unable to trace Marx's use of the term 'pure commodity' in the particular pages (141, 145, 166–7) of the Penguin edition of the *Grundrisse* to which Giddens refers the reader.

33. Marx, *Capital*, Volume I, p. 186. Later, Marx observes: 'Value exists only in use-values, in things, if we leave aside its purely symbolic representations in tokens.' (Ibid., p. 310.)

34. Was Sica right then? It certainly appears that one does not have to read very far in the work of Parsons in order to assemble most of the key elements of Giddens' 'fresh characterisation of modernity', plus much else besides.

Take, for example, a single, 24-page article, republished as chapter 9 of *Social Systems and the Evolution of Action Theory* (New York 1977). A cursory reading of this chapter reveals that the 'media of interchange' which Giddens calls 'symbolic tokens' are uncannily similar to what Parsons here calls the 'generalized symbolic media of interchange'. For Parsons too asserts that these symbolic media define 'the limits of such areas within which extension of systems of transaction can develop and proliferate'. (Ibid., p. 209.) Parsons too starts with money, which he too defines in terms of credit and debt. Parsons too argues for the existence of other generalized symbolic media, and his first port of call is the only other 'symbolic token' mentioned by Giddens – namely political legitimacy. However, while Giddens leaves the idea hanging at this point, Parsons goes on to specify two further media: 'influence' and 'value-commitment'. Any idea that this marks a point of real difference, however, is almost immediately undermined by Parsons' discussions of these. The first – illustrated by the example of 'doctor's orders' – is bound up with the legitimacy derived from expert knowledge. And the second is explicitly stated to be 'anchored in the fiduciary system' – that is, bound up with 'trust'.

No doubt Giddens would wish to assert that these apparent similarities mask underlying differences of real significance. But the fact remains that by defining money and political legitimacy as symbolic tokens, and by following this up with discussions of expert knowledge and trust, he has reproduced willy-nilly the fourfold Parsonian template. And a substantial case would have to be made in order to establish that his own problematic involves a real move beyond Parsons' schema, rather than being simply the cumulative result of that 'redefinitional ingenuity' of which Sica accuses him.

In fact, the charge could be widened yet further. One of the most familiar criticisms of Parsonian structural functionalism was that its 'static bias' rendered it incapable of grasping processes of historical change. By contrast, a perceived strength of Giddens' structuration theory is that by re-interpolating the dimension of time into sociological analysis, it not only addressed this problem but also revealed that the *stable reproduction* of social orders needed equally to be understood as a dynamic process. One might therefore initially view with some surprise the spectacle of Parsons himself carrying out a similar interpolation. Yet this is what he does in the same article we have been discussing. For he goes out of his way to underline that his conception of symbolic media (which later reappears as Giddens' 'symbolic tokens') 'introduces an element of dynamic into the analysis of social relationships and processes'. (Ibid., p. 208.) He states his belief that working this dynamic conception of media into his general theory 'goes far, it seems to me, to refute the frequent allegations that this type of structural analysis is inherently plagued with a static bias'. (Ibid., p. 209.) And finally, in a stroke which threatens to deprive structuration theory of one of its principal claims to originality, he adds: 'Let me, then, again insist that under the category of dynamic I mean to include both equili-brating processes and processes of structural change.' The reader who absorbs the significance of these remarks will perhaps then be less surprised, though no less intrigued, when, ten pages later, Parsons rises to a passable formulation of what later reappears as the central focus of structuration theory under the heading of 'the duality of structure'.

35. Marx, *Capital*, Volume I, p. 209.

36. Marx, *Grundrisse*, p. 524.

37. Whether in fact Giddens ever understood these points is difficult to judge. On the one hand, he once rightly identified 'the objec-tives of [*Capital*] as a whole [as being] to document this metamorphosis of human relationships into phenomena of the market'. (*Capitalism and Modern Social Theory*, p. 64.) Indeed, in 1981, he was still claiming that Marx, by distinguishing between use-value and exchange-value, 'demonstrates how money expresses and makes possible the disembedding of social rela-tionships'. (*A Contemporary Critique of Historical Materialism, Volume 1: Power, Property and the State*, London 1981, p. 115.) On the other hand, even in his major exposition of Marx in 1971, an exposition which aims to provide 'a concise yet comprehensive analysis of [Marx's] sociological ideas' (*Capitalism and Modern Social Theory*, p. vii), the arguably central theme of fetishism is not brought out. The theory of value itself is treated as part of the theory of surplus value, and, following Meek, is merged with the antecedent theories of Smith and Ricardo – whom Marx had criticised for fetishising the value-creating properties of labour. The underlying confusions which this generates work their way rapidly to the sur-face of the text in the form of some very basic misunderstandings indeed. Giddens argues, for example, that 'both exchange-value *and use-value* must be directly related to the *amount* of labour embodied in the production of a commodity.' (Ibid., p. 46 – emphases added.) Marx, of course, argued no such thing.

Giddens could potentially have covered himself in *The Consequences of Modernity* by arguing that the ontological depth to capitalist social relations proposed by Marx is itself illusory, together with the apparent need which it implies for a social theory of value. This was the position taken by Weber *en route* to his formulation of an alternative, marginalist method of explanation: 'It has proved possible entirely to avoid the controversial concept of "value"'. (See *Economy and Society: An Outline of Interpretive Sociology*, Volume I, ed. G. Roth and C. Wittich, Berkeley, CA, 1978, p. 63.) Giddens, however, does not attempt this move.

38.   'Author's Introduction', reprinted in Weber, *The Protestant Ethic*, p. 16.

39.   Weber, *Economy and Society*, Volume II, p. 957.

40.   'Science as a Vocation', in *From Max Weber*, ed. H. Gerth and C. Wright Mills, London 1948, p. 139.

41.   Weber, *The Protestant Ethic*, pp. 18–22.

42.   'Science contributes to the technology of controlling life by calculating external objects as well as man's activity . . . [use of it, however,] must take into the bargain the [unpredictable] subsidiary consequences which according to all experience will occur . . . etc.' *From Max Weber*, pp. 150–1.

43.   Weber, *Economy and Society*, Volume I, p. 30. He continues by adding: 'One of the most important aspects of the process of "rationalization" of action is the substitution for the unthinking acceptance of ancient custom, of deliberate adaptation.'

44.   Weber, *The Protestant Ethic*, pp. 78 and 26.

45.   It enables Weber to argue simultaneously that 'even the knowledge of the most certain proposition of our theoretical sciences . . . is . . . a product of culture' *and* that 'a systematically correct scientific proof in the social sciences . . . must be acknowledged as correct even by a Chinese.' See Weber, *The Methodology of the Social Sciences*, pp. 55 and 58.

46.   To give just three more examples: Boyne chides Giddens for misrepresenting Foucault and Derrida (see 'Power-Knowledge

and Social Theory: The Systematic Misrepresentation of French Social Theory in the Work of Anthony Giddens', in Bryant and Jary, eds, *Anthony Giddens: Critical Assessments*, Volume I); Gane ('Anthony Giddens and the Crisis in Social Theory', in ibid.) argues that Giddens' invocation of Durkheim in *New Rules* is curious in a text which 'smacked precisely of the very kind of philosophical subjectivism that Durkheim set out to criticise' (ibid., p. 195); but perhaps most damaging of all is Ian Craib's critique of 'Giddens' misuse or misrepresentation of psychoanalysis'. Not only, says Craib, does Giddens' use of Freud lose 'the complexity of the original'; but worse, his crucial category of 'ontological security' is lifted from the work of Laing, where, however, it entails 'exactly the opposite of Giddens' propositions'. Similarly, of the object-relations school of psychoanalysis (including Winnicott) on whom Giddens places such weight, Craib observes: 'Giddens does not understand these writers'. (See I. Craib, 'The Problem with People', in ibid., Volume II, pp. 353, 357 and 356 respectively.)

47.   For a brief overview of Clausewitz's work, see M. Howard, *Clausewitz*, Oxford 1983. Howard apparently has no difficulty in seeing that Clausewitz's argument about total war, formulated in the aftermath of the French Revolutionary and Napoleonic Wars, was rooted principally in a socio-political analysis of the impact of new democratic forms of legitimation on the dynamics of military conflict. For this reason, its basic insight would in fact be vindicated, not rendered obsolete, by the process of industrialisation. Thus the Second World War, says Howard, was 'a conflict that lent itself at every level to a Clausewitzian analysis'. Meanwhile, elements of Clausewitz's work also supply 'a depressingly accurate description of contemporary nuclear strategy', and in sum, 'all the considerations analysed by Clausewitz would be as relevant today as they were a century and a half . . . ago.' See ibid., pp. 69, 70 and 72.

48. C. von Clausewitz, *On War*, ed. and trans. M. Howard and P. Paret, Princeton, NJ, 1984, p. 605.

49. '[T]he economists', writes Marx, 'say that people place in a thing (money) the faith which they do not place in each other. But why do they have faith in the thing?' *Grundrisse*, p. 160.

50. See *Consequences*, pp. 72, 56, 14, 73 and 76 respectively. In fact, on page 57, Giddens announces that 'capitalist economic life is only in a few respects confined to the boundaries of specific social systems' – a usage of the latter term which somewhat undercuts his claim that it releases us from the focus on 'bounded entities'.

51. A similar point has been well made by Ian Craib. See 'The Problem with People', pp. 352–3.

52. This strong claim is actually not just a corner Giddens is forced into at a late stage in his argument. He had already formulated it explicitly in *Central Problems in Social Theory*, back in 1979: 'The most basic sense of mediation is that involved in the 'binding' of time and space themselves, *the very essence of social reproduction*.' (See *Central Problems*, p. 103, emphasis added.)

53. Marx, *Grundrisse*, p. 164.

54. Ibid., p. 163.

55. *The German Ideology*, in K. Marx and F. Engels, *Collected Works*, Volume V, trans. C. Dutt, W. Lough and C. Magill, Moscow 1976, p. 87.

56. Sayer, *Capitalism and Modernity*, p. 58.

57. Marx, *Grundrisse*, p. 84.

58. K. Polanyi, *The Great Transformation: The Political and Economic Origins of Our Time*, Boston 1957, p. 57.

59. While *Consequences* redefines 'disembedding' without mentioning Polanyi, *The Nation-State and Violence* contains a brief discussion (on p. 67) of Polanyi without, however, mentioning 'disembedding'.

60. The same could be said of the even greater familiarity of the term which plays the same role in a later work: 'runaway world'. It seems almost futile to recall that *that* phrase was used thirty

years ago by Marshall McLuhan. For the real point is exactly that the image is by now such a commonplace that it could have come from anywhere. See, however, for an example, *Culture is Our Business*, extracted in *Essential McLuhan*, ed. E. McLuhan and F. Zingrone, New York 1995, p. 36.

61. Marx, *Capital*, Volume I, p. 392.

62. How, he wonders on page 165, given the enormous material inequalities and finite resources of the contemporary world, could 'post-scarcity' be a realistic goal? 'Let us ask instead, *what other alternative is there* for a world which does not pursue a self-destructive path?'

63. Emphasis added.

64. Weber, *The Protestant Ethic*, p. 182.

5. CONCLUSION: THE COLLAPSING TEMPLE OF GLOBALISATION THEORY

1. I have inferred the rules of this game from two sources: D. Jary and J. Jary, 'The Transformations of Anthony Giddens', reprinted in C. Bryant and D. Jary, eds, *Anthony Giddens: Critical Assessments* (4 vols), Volume IV, London 1997; and, secondarily, the section entitled 'Evaluating Giddens' *Oeuvre*', in Bryant and Jary's 'General Introduction' to Volume I of the same work.

2. I. Craib, 'The Problem with People', in ibid., Volume II, pp. 356 and 358.

3. Z. Bauman, *Globalization: The Human Consequences*, Cambridge 1998, p. 57.

4. Ibid., p. 70.

5. 'Russia', excerpted in M.G. Forsyth, H. Keens-Soper and P. Savigear, eds, *The Theory of International Relations: Selected Texts from Gentili to Treitschke*, London 1970, p. 309.

Bibliography

Albrow, M., *The Global Age*, Cambridge 1996.

Anderson, B., *Language and Power: Exploring Political Cultures in Indonesia*, Ithaca, NY, and London 1990.

Anderson, B., *Imagined Communities: Reflections on the Origin and Spread of Nationalism*, 2nd edn, London 1991.

Anderson, P., 'Max Weber and Ernest Gellner', in *A Zone of Engagement*, London 1992.

Aristotle, *The Politics of Aristotle*, trans. E. Barker, Oxford 1946.

Aveni, A., *Empires of Time: Calendars, Clocks and Cultures*, London 1990.

Bauman, Z., *Intimations of Postmodernity*, London 1992.

Bauman, Z., *Globalization: The Human Consequences*, Cambridge 1998.

Beck, U., *Risk Society: Towards a New Modernity*, trans. M. Ritter, London 1992.

Berman, M., *All That is Solid Melts into Air*, London 1983.

Bleicher, J. and Featherstone, M., 'Historical Materialism Today: An Interview with Anthony Giddens', in C. Bryant and D. Jary, eds, *Anthony Giddens: Critical Assessments*, Volume I, London 1997.

Bloch, M., 'The Past and the Present in the Present', *Man* (NS), 12, 1977.

Bohannan, P., 'Concepts of Time Among the Tiv of Nigeria', *Southwestern Journal of Anthropology*, 9 (3), 1953.

Bourdieu, P., 'The Attitude of the Algerian Peasant toward Time', in J.

Pitt-Rivers, ed., *Mediterranean Countrymen: Essays in the Social Anthropology of the Mediterranean*, Paris 1963.

Bourne, K., *The Foreign Policy of Victorian England 1830–1902*, Oxford 1970.

Boyne, R., 'Power-Knowledge and Social Theory: The Systematic Misrepresentation of French Social Theory in the Work of Anthony Giddens', in C. Bryant and D. Jary, eds, *Anthony Giddens: Critical Assessments*, Volume I, London 1997.

Bryant, C. and Jary, D., eds, *Anthony Giddens: Critical Assessments* (4 vols), London 1997.

Bryant, C. and Jary, D., 'General Introduction', in C. Bryant and D. Jary, eds, *Anthony Giddens: Critical Assessments*, Volume I, London 1997.

Butterfield, H., 'The Tragic Element in Modern International Conflict', in *History and Human Relations*, London 1951.

Clark, I., *Globalization and International Relations Theory*, Oxford 1999.

Clark, J., C. Modgil and S. Modgil, eds, *Anthony Giddens: Consensus and Controversy*, Basingstoke 1990.

Clausewitz, C. von, *On War*, ed. and trans. M. Howard and P. Paret, Princeton, NJ, 1989.

Clegg, S., 'How to Become an Internationally Famous British Social Theorist', in C. Bryant and D. Jary, eds, *Anthony Giddens: Critical Assessments*, Volume I, London 1997.

Cobden, R., 'Russia', excerpted in M.G. Forsyth, H. Keens-Soper and P. Savigear, eds, *The Theory of International Relations: Selected Texts from Gentili to Treitschke*, London 1970.

Craib, I., 'The Problem with People', in C. Bryant and D. Jary, eds, *Anthony Giddens: Critical Assessments*, Volume II, London 1997.

Donelan, M., 'The Political Theorists and International Relations', in M. Donelan, ed., *The Reason of States: A Study in International Political Theory*, London 1978.

Evans-Pritchard, E., 'Nuer Time-Reckoning', *Africa*, 12, 1939.

Featherstone, M., Lash, S. and Robertson, R., eds, *Global Modernities*, London 1995.

Fraser, J.T., ed., *The Voices of Time: A Cooperative Survey of Man's Views of Time as Expressed by the Sciences and by the Humanities*, London 1968.

French Smith, M., 'Bloody Time and Bloody Scarcity: Capitalism, Authority, and the Transformation of Temporal Experience in a Papua New Guinea Village', *American Ethnologist*, 9, 1982.

Gallagher, J. and Robinson, R., 'The Imperialism of Free Trade', *Economic History Review*, Second Series, VI (I), 1953. (Reprinted in A. Shaw, ed., *Great Britain and the Colonies 1815–1865*, London 1970.)

Gane, M., 'Anthony Giddens and the Crisis in Social Theory', in C. Bryant and D. Jary, eds, *Anthony Giddens: Critical Assessments*, Volume I, London 1997.

Geertz, C., 'Person, Time and Conduct in Bali' (1963), reprinted in *The Interpretation of Cultures*, London 1993.

Giddens, A., *Capitalism and Modern Social Theory*, Cambridge 1971.

Giddens, A., *Central Problems in Social Theory*, London 1979.

Giddens, A., *A Contemporary Critique of Historical Materialism. Volume 1: Power, Property and the State*, London 1981.

Giddens, A., *The Constitution of Society*, Cambridge 1984.

Giddens, A., *The Nation-State and Violence*, Cambridge 1985.

Giddens, A., *The Consequences of Modernity*, Cambridge 1990.

Giddens, A., *Runaway World: How Globalisation is Reshaping Our Lives*, London 1999.

Goldstein, L., *The Social and Cultural Roots of Linear Perspective*, Minneapolis, MN, 1988.

Gross, L., 'The Peace of Westphalia 1648–1948', *The American Journal of International Law*, 42, 1948.

Hansen, L., 'R.B.J. Walker and International Relations: Deconstructing a Discipline', in I. Neumann and O. Wæver, eds, *The Future of International Relations: Masters in the Making*, London 1997.

Hassard, J., ed., *The Sociology of Time*, London 1990.

Held, D. and McGrew, A., 'The End of the Old Order? Globalization and the Prospects for World Order', *Review of International Studies*, 24, Special Issue, December 1998.

Held, D., McGrew, A., Goldblatt, D. and Perraton, J., *Global Transformations: Politics, Economics, Culture*, Cambridge 1999.

Hobsbawm, E.J., *Industry and Empire*, Harmondsworth 1968.

Hoogvelt, A., *Globalisation and the Postcolonial World: The New Political Economy of Development*, Basingstoke 1997.

Howard, M., *Clausewitz*, Oxford 1983.

Jary, D. and Jary, J., 'The Transformations of Anthony Giddens', in C. Bryant and D. Jary, eds, *Anthony Giddens: Critical Assessments*, Volume IV, London 1997.

Jones, R., 'The Responsibility to Educate', *Review of International Studies*, 20, 1994.

Krasner, S., 'Westphalia and All That', in J. Goldstein and R. Keohane, eds, *Ideas and Foreign Policy: Beliefs, Institutions and Political Change*, New York 1993.

Le Goff, J., *Time, Work and Culture in the Middle Ages*, Chicago, IL, 1980.

Lowe, D., *History of Bourgeois Perception*, Brighton 1982.

Löwith, K., *Max Weber and Karl Marx*, ed. T. Bottomore and W. Outhwaite, London 1982.

McLuhan, M., *Essential McLuhan*, ed. E. McLuhan and F. Zingrone, New York 1995.

Marx, K., *Grundrisse*, trans. M. Nicolaus, Harmondsworth 1973.

Marx, K., *Early Writings*, trans. R. Livingstone and G. Benton, Harmondsworth 1975.

Marx, K., *Capital*, Volume I, Harmondsworth 1976.

Marx, K., *The German Ideology*, in K. Marx and F. Engels, *Collected Works*, Volume V, trans. C. Dutt, W. Lough and C. Magill, Moscow 1976.

Marx, K., *Readings from Karl Marx*, ed. D. Sayer, London 1989.

Marx, K. and Engels, F., *Correspondence 1846–1895*, ed. and trans. D. Torr, London 1934.

Mills, C. Wright, *The Sociological Imagination*, Oxford 1959.

Mumford, L., *Technics and Civilization*, London 1934.

Needham, J., 'Time and Eastern Man', in *The Grand Titration: Science and Society in East and West*, London 1969.

Nietzsche, F., *The Gay Science*, trans. W. Kaufmann, New York 1974.

Notes

1. INTRODUCTION: THE PROBLEM OF GLOBALISATION THEORY

1. A. Giddens, *The Consequences of Modernity*, Cambridge 1990, p. 52.
2. The lectures were later published as *Runaway World: How Globalization is Reshaping Our Lives*, London 1999.
3. 26 October 1997.
4. M. Albrow, *The Global Age*, Cambridge 1996, p. 4.
5. M. Featherstone and S. Lash, 'Globalization, Modernity and the Spatialization of Social Theory: An Introduction', in M. Featherstone, S. Lash and R. Robertson, eds, *Global Modernities*, London 1995, p. 1.
6. Z. Bauman, *Globalization: The Human Consequences*, Cambridge 1998, p. 15.
7. Ibid., pp. 12 and 15.
8. Featherstone and Lash, 'Globalization, Modernity', in Featherstone et al. (eds), *Global Modernities*, p. 1.
9. M. Waters, *Globalization*, London 1995, p. 1.
10. Giddens, *Consequences*, p. 64.
11. See, for example, his discussion of the category of 'labour' in the 1857 'General Introduction', *Grundrisse*, trans. M. Nicolaus, Harmondsworth 1973, pp. 103ff.

12.   A. Hoogvelt, *Globalisation and the Postcolonial World: The New Political Economy of Development*, Basingstoke 1997, p. 121. This announcement comes at the end of a brief discussion of Giddens' work, specifically *The Consequences of Modernity*.

13.   Lewis Mumford's observation that 'no two cultures live conceptually in the same kind of time and space' was uncontroversial when it was penned in 1934. (See his *Technics and Civilization*, London 1934, p. 18.) Since then it has been filled out by a wealth of anthropological and other studies. Some of the more celebrated of these include: E. Evans-Pritchard's 'Nuer Time-Reckoning' (*Africa*, 12, 1939); Paul Bohannan's 'Concepts of Time Among the Tiv of Nigeria' (*Southwestern Journal of Anthropology*, 9 (3), 1953, 251–62); Pierre Bourdieu's 'The Attitude of the Algerian Peasant toward Time' (in S. Pitt-Rivers, ed., *Mediterranean Countrymen: Essays in the Social Anthropology of the Mediterranean*, Paris 1963); Marc Bloch's 'The Past and the Present in the Present' (*Man* (NS), 12, 1977, 278–92); Clifford Geertz's 'Person, Time and Conduct in Bali' (1963, reprinted in his *The Interpretation of Cultures*, London 1993); Jacques Le Goff's *Time, Work and Culture in the Middle Ages* (Chicago 1980); various works of Eviatar Zerubavel, Maurice Godelier, and so on.

Full-length cross-cultural studies of time include A. Aveni, *Empires of Time: Calendars, Clocks and Cultures*, London 1990; J.T. Fraser, ed., *The Voices of Time: A Cooperative Survey of Man's Views of Time as Expressed by the Sciences and by the Humanities*, London 1968; and G.J. Whitrow, *Time in History: Views of Time from Prehistory to the Present Day*, Oxford 1988.

Examples of major contributions from different disciplines include two volumes by Robert David Sack (*Conceptions of Space in Social Thought: A Geographic Perspective*, London 1980, and *Human Territoriality: Its Theory and History*, Cambridge 1986); Leonard Goldstein's *The Social and Cultural Roots of Linear Perspective*, Minneapolis 1988; Henry Rutz, ed., *The Politics of Time*, Washington 1992; J. Hassard, ed., *The Sociology of Time*, London

Parsons, T., *Social Systems and the Evolution of Action Theory*, New York 1977.

Polanyi, K., *The Great Transformation: The Political and Economic Origins of Our Time*, Boston 1957.

Poulantzas, N., *State, Power, Socialism*, London 1978.

Rabb, T., ed., *The Thirty Years' War: Problems of Motive, Extent, and Effect*, Boston 1964.

Robertson, R., *Globalization: Social Theory and Global Culture*, London 1992.

Robertson, R., 'Glocalization: Time-Space and Homogeneity-Heterogeneity', in M. Featherstone, S. Lash and R. Robertson, eds, *Global Modernities*, London 1995.

Rosenberg, J., *The Empire of Civil Society: A Critique of the Realist Theory of International Relations*, London 1994.

Rosenberg, J., 'The International Imagination: IR Theory and Classic Social Analysis', *Millennium* 23 (1), Spring 1994.

Rutz, H., ed., *The Politics of Time*, Washington 1992.

Sack, R.D., *Conceptions of Space in Social Thought: A Geographic Perspective*, London 1980.

Sack, R.D., *Human Territoriality: Its Theory and History*, Cambridge 1986.

Sayer, D., 'The Critique of Politics and Political Economy: Capitalism, Communism and the State in Marx's Writings of the mid-1840s', *Sociological Review*, 33 (2), 1985.

Sayer, D., *Capitalism and Modernity: An Excursus on Marx and Weber*, London 1991.

Sayer, D., 'Reinventing the Wheel: Anthony Giddens, Karl Marx and Social Change', in J. Clark, C. Modgil and S. Modgil, eds, *Anthony Giddens: Consensus and Controversy*, London 1991.

Scholte, J.A., 'Globalisation: Prospects for a Paradigm Shift', in M. Shaw, ed., *Politics and Globalisation*, London 1999.

Scholte, J.A., *Globalization: A Critical Introduction*, Basingstoke 2000.

Sica, A., 'The California–Massachusetts Strain in Structuration Theory', in C. Bryant and D. Jary, eds, *Anthony Giddens: Critical Assessments*, Volume I, London 1997.

Stedman Jones, G., 'The History of US Imperialism', in R. Blackburn, ed., *Ideology in Social Science: Readings in Critical Social Theory*, London 1972.

Symcox, G., ed., *War, Diplomacy and Imperialism, 1618–1763: Selected Documents*, London 1974.

Thompson, E.P., 'Time, Work-Discipline and Industrial Capitalism', *Past and Present*, 38, 1967 (reprinted in *Customs in Common*, London 1991).

Turner, B., 'Weber, Giddens and Modernity', in C. Bryant and D. Jary, eds, *Anthony Giddens: Critical Assessments*, Volume IV, London 1997.

Walker, R.B.J., *Inside/Outside: International Relations as Political Theory*, Cambridge 1993.

Walker, R.B.J., 'On Pedagogical Responsibility: A Response to Roy Jones', *Review of International Studies*, 20, 1994.

Walker, R.B.J., 'International Relations and the Concept of the Political', in K. Booth and S. Smith, eds, *International Relations Theory Today*, Cambridge 1995.

Waltz, K.N., *Theory of International Politics*, New York 1979.

Waters, M., *Globalization*, London 1995.

Weber, M., *From Max Weber*, ed. H. Gerth and C. Wright Mills, London 1948.

Weber, M., *The Methodology of the Social Sciences*, trans. and ed. E. Shills and H. Finch, New York 1949.

Weber, M., *Economy and Society: An Outline of Interpretive Sociology*, 2 vols, ed. G. Roth and C. Wittich, Berkeley, CA, 1978.

Weber, M., *The Protestant Ethic and the Spirit of Capitalism*, trans. T. Parsons, London 1984.

Wedgwood, C.V., *The Thirty Years War*, London 1938.

Whitrow, G., *Time in History: Views of Time from Prehistory to the Present Day*, Oxford 1988.

Wight, M., 'Why is There No International Theory?' in H. Butterfield and M. Wight, eds, *Diplomatic Investigations*, London 1966.

Wolf, E., *Europe and the People Without History*, Berkeley, CA, 1982.

Woodward, D., 'Reality, Symbolism, Time, and Space in Medieval
  World Maps', *Annals of the Association of American Geographers*, 75
  (4), 1985.
Youngs, G., *International Relations in a Global Age: A Conceptual Challenge*,
  Cambridge 1999.

Index

abstractions 63–4, 137
abstract systems 112, 114, 134, 149, 161
  and kinship 138, 140
  spatio-temporal properties 122, 145
  see also expert systems; symbolic tokens
Albrow, Martin 88
anarchy 80
Anderson, Benedict 50, 61–2, 63, 64, 65, 98
Anderson, Perry 62

Bauman, Zygmunt 11, 88, 100, 164–5
Beck, Ulrich 183n
Berman, Marshall 95
bureaucracy 112–13

capitalism 19, 35–6, 116–17
  and modernity 92, 96
  spatio-temporal analysis 32–3, 42

classical social theory 8, 63, 87
  expert systems 108–10
  individuals 136–7
  modernity 89, 92–3, 94–100, 145, 147
  symbolic tokens 104–8
Classic Social Analysis 8
Clausewitz, C. von 113–14, 189n
Cobden, Richard 33, 165
community 134–5, 149
cotton industry 31–3, 34–5
Craib, Ian 159–60

deterritorialisation 21–2
dialectics 148–9
differentiation 139–40
difficulty 47, 84
disembedding 117, 122–3, 139, 146, 162
  mechanisms 102–4
  and re-embedding 149, 150–51
Donelan, Michael 66–7, 68, 73
double-edged phenomenon 94, 95

Durkheim, Emile 92, 94–5

ecological crisis 98
embedded 151
evolutionism 94–5, 99
expert systems 102, 103, 108–10,
    112, 113, 122

fragmentation 80, 82
friendship 135–6, 137

Gellner, Ernest 62
Gemeinschaft 135, 141
generality 74–5
    Marx 71–3
    Walker 73
Gesellschaft 135, 141
Giddens, Anthony 7, 13, 87–91,
    132–4, 157–64
    bureaucracy 112–13
    on Clausewitz 113–14
    dialectics of space and time
        147–55
    as expert 114–15
    expert systems 102, 108–10, 112,
        113
    globalisation 1, 2, 118–21
    modernity 91–100, 116–18
    risk and ontological security
        141–7
    symbolic tokens 102, 104–8
    time-space distantiation 101–2,
        115–16, 121–5, 132
    transformation of intimacy
        134–41

trust 102, 103–4, 125–31
globalisation 1–4, 19, 21–2
    Giddens 118–21, 153
globalisation theory 2–3, 4
    and International Relations
        9–15
globality 26

Hansen, Lene 67, 176n
Harvey, David 42
Held, David 29, 46, 88
historical materialism 3, 178–9n
history
    Giddens 100
    Walker 53–4, 60, 68, 81
Hoogvelt, Ankie 4, 118

impersonality 149, 151–2
individuals 136–7
industrialisation 96
industrialism 92, 116, 117
institutions 94, 96–7
international 65–85, 178n
    Walker 50, 57
internationalisation 21
International Relations 9–15,
    27–8, 50, 66
    Walker 48–9, 58–9, 68, 69
intimacy 134–41, 149, 151–2
inverted Robinsonades 73, 82

Jones, Gareth Stedman 31
Jones, Roy 67

King Cotton 31–3, 34–5

kinship 129, 130, 135, 138, 140
knowledge *see* social knowledge

liberalisation 21
locality 129–30, 150–51
Lowe, Donald 6, 32, 64

McGrew, Anthony 29
Marx, Karl 8, 82
    abstractions 63, 81, 137
    capitalism 92, 118
    cotton industry 33, 34–5
    generality and particularity
        71–3, 74, 75
    historical materialism 3
    international 50
    modernity 94, 95, 96, 97, 100,
        147, 148
    money 104–8, 187n
    production 75–6, 80
    Robinsonades 68, 69–71
    sovereignty 20, 35–7
methodological territorialism 9,
    30–32, 39
Mills, C. Wright 8
modernisation 21
modernity 61, 63
    classical social theory 92–100,
        109, 147
    Giddens 88–9, 91–2, 104, 145,
        161–2
        disembedding mechanisms
            122
        institutional analysis 90,
            116–18

juggernaut imagery 147–8
    and risk 143
    time-space distantiation 101
    Walker 46, 53, 60
money 102, 104–8

nationalism 62
new social movements 88, 89
Nietzsche, Friedrich 65

ontological security 126–9, 159–60
    and risk 143–7
    spatio-temporal conditions 132,
        133, 137, 162
other 51, 52–3, 56

Parsons, Talcott 99, 108, 160,
    185–7n
particularity 51, 52, 56, 74–5
    Marx 71–3
    Walker 73
Polanyi, Karl 139
polis 68, 83–4
political 37, 76–8
postinternational system 10
Poulantzas, Nicos 6, 38, 40, 41,
    42–3, 63, 176n

rational abstraction 74, 75–6
rationalisation 92, 96, 109–10,
    111–12
reason 111–12
re-embedding 123, 149, 150–51
reflexivity 94, 97–8, 99, 117, 153
religious cosmology 130

risk 141–7, 150
Robertson, Roland 88
Robinsonades 68, 69–71, 73, 82

Sack, Robert David 6, 7
Sayer, Derek 137, 181–2n
Scholte, Jan Aart 7, 14, 17–20
    globalisation 21–7
    International Relations 27–8
    methodological territorialism 9,
        31–2, 33
    supraterritorality 33–4, 39,
        163–4
    Westphalian System 30–31, 41–2
self 51, 52–3, 56
sexual relations 135, 136
slavery 31, 33, 35, 179n
social evolutionism 94–5, 99
social knowledge 93
    reflexivity 94, 97–8, 99, 153
sovereignty 28–9, 35–8, 40, 62–3,
    64
    Walker 46, 54–61, 83, 176n
space 4–7, 13, 14, 163–5
    Poulantzas 42–3, 176n
    Scholte 19, 21, 22–4, 39
    Walker 45–6, 47–8, 50, 63, 64–5,
        82, 84
    and modernity 55, 56–8
    ontological assumptions 51,
        53–4
    see also time-space distantiation
structuration theory 186–7n
supraterritoriality 9, 17, 19–20,
    25–6, 31–3, 39

surveillance 116
symbolic tokens 102, 104–8, 122,
    185–6n

temporal accelerations 47, 48, 163
territorialism 23–4, 30–32
time 4–7, 14, 24–5, 42, 163–5
    Walker 48, 51, 53–4, 56–7, 163
time-space distantiation 87, 89,
    93–4, 130–31, 132, 145
    and classical social theory 97
    and globalisation 119–21, 163
    implosion 90, 101–2, 115–16,
        117, 121–2, 160–61, 162
    and trust 127, 129–30
Tönnies, Ferdinand 135
totalitarianism 98
tradition 130
transborder 32–3
transworld simultaneity 32–3
trust 102, 103–4, 122–3, 124, 144
    and ontological security 125–31,
        144
Weber 110

universalisation 21
universality 26, 51, 52, 56
utopian realism 89

Walker, Rob 7–8, 11, 45–50, 163–4
    international 65, 67–8, 69,
        70–71, 73, 80, 82, 83–4
    ontological assumptions 50–54
    space 63, 64–5
    space and modernity 54–61

Wallerstein, Immanuel 27
Waters, Malcolm 9
Weber, Max 8, 45, 61, 154
    bureaucracy 113
    expert systems 108–10
    modernity 92, 95, 96, 97–8, 100,
        147
    nationalism 62

rationalisation 64, 111–12
Westernisation 21
Westphalian System 10, 15, 19–20,
    27–43
Wight, Martin 66
World Systems Theory 27

Youngs, Gillian 46